ACTIVE
READING
CLASSROOMS

Strategies That Build
Language Comprehension and
Word Recognition Skills

Jennifer Kelly

Pembroke Publishers Limited

For my husband Steve. You inspire me every single day.

© 2023 Pembroke Publishers
538 Hood Road
Markham, Ontario, Canada L3R 3K9
www.pembrokepublishers.com

Funded by the Government of Canada
Financé par le gouvernement du Canada | Canada

Library and Archives Canada Cataloguing in Publication

Title: Active reading classrooms: strategies that build language comprehension and word recognition skills / Jennifer Kelly.

Names: Kelly, Jennifer (Jennifer Lynn), author.

Description: Includes bibliographical references and index.

Identifiers: Canadiana (print) 20230483208 | Canadiana (ebook) 20230483216 | ISBN 9781551383651 (softcover) | ISBN 9781551389646 (PDF)

Subjects: LCSH: Reading (Elementary) | LCSH: Reading comprehension—Study and teaching (Elementary) | LCSH: Word recognition—Study and teaching (Elementary)

Classification: LCC LB1573 .K45 2023 | DDC 372.4—dc23

Editor: David Kilgour
Cover Design: John Zehethofer
Typesetting: Jay Tee Graphics Ltd.

Printed and bound in Canada
9 8 7 6 5 4 3 2 1

Contents

Introduction

My own primary classrooms and the other classrooms I have had the privilege to be a part of over the past twenty-three years have shaped my thinking about literacy instruction and how important it is to put students and their thinking concretely at the centre of my teaching. The more classrooms I am in and the more teachers I meet, the more in awe I am of educators in this profession and their deep commitment to ongoing professional learning. It is my greatest hope that this book reinforces the important work teachers are doing every day, gives teachers tools to further engage students in meaningful ways, and opens up conversation among colleagues. It is my honor to write this book for teachers.

I remember the exact time in my life when I realized the power of a story. I was a student reading *Lord of the Flies*, by William Golding, in my grade 8 English Language Arts class. It was the first time I had heard about symbolism, and I was beyond fascinated. I began to understand the power of words and phrases, not only to the reader but as an interaction between the reader and the author. I entered into a relationship with Golding as I was guided through the story and what the story meant to me as a reader. The place of understanding was between me and the text I was reading, a swirling space of words, thoughts, ideas, and theories. That was powerful. As Proust wrote, "the heart of the reading act [is] going beyond the wisdom of the author to discover one's own." This book highlights the complexity of the different components of reading as detailed by current research, but with fairly simple ways to bring those theories into the classroom through instructional strategies.

I chose to write this book to both figuratively and literally work alongside teachers as they unpack current reading research and discover what ways they can broaden reading instruction to support our students. I appreciate all the research Nell Duke and Kelly Cartwright have put into building the Active View of Reading model that this book is based on and I have put all that research into practical examples that teachers can use in their classrooms immediately.

We want our students to dive into texts, learn new ways of making sense of their world, and see themselves as readers. I've leaned heavily on a question posed by Aukerman and Schuldt (2021), as I wrote this book: "How can reading instruction best help students develop and flourish as literate beings in the ways that matter the most?" (p. 86).

This book is structured as a journey through the different components of the Active View of Reading model. I describe each component of reading instruction to give information about how it supports reading development, and then follow up with practical instructional activities you can try out with your students. Most of the strategies and activities will continue to benefit students into intermediate grades, but the word recognition components will benefit primary students until they are proficient with those foundational skills. Therefore, this book is written for teachers of kindergarten to later elementary (grade 5 or 6), with a focus on differentiating instruction to meet our students where they are in their learning journey.

Although the classroom activities described are far from exhaustive, they can provide some direction in the different components of the Active View of Reading. The activities are meant to be used repeatedly while changing the content or the context of learning. In addition, my hope is that teachers try out different instructional strategies and notice how their students respond. When teachers take an inquiry approach to instruction, they may find out what works for them, their students, and their diverse contexts.

1

The Active View of Reading

Introduction to the Active View of Reading Model

Recent trends in teaching reading are gaining traction in the news, in staffrooms, and among reading researchers. There are many different opinions about what teachers should focus on with early readers and students who are struggling with reading. However, it is our teachers who are at the forefront of the struggle. We are the ones working with our students every day and we are the ones who can't sleep at night as we think about why some of our students are not reading. We need to be at the centre of the conversations about reading instruction because, simply, we are the ones teaching reading.

A lot of the conversation recently is about the Science of Reading. Although there are many different definitions and understanding about what that term refers to, many teachers agree that it involves being systematic and explicit about how we teach reading. The more we learn about the reading brain, the more we understand how students are processing information and we use that knowledge when teaching reading. When students are not processing information in a way that makes sense to us, then we need to explore different ways of supporting them in how they are processing information.

I think teachers will agree that we all want to do what will get the greatest number of our students to read.

There are some instructional strategies that most students benefit from in the form of systematic instruction. But there are some students who need those steps to be made explicit in order to learn how to read. I think teachers will agree that we all want to do what will get the greatest number of our students to read. We can call it whatever we want, but it is just putting our students at the centre of our practice.

A popular reading model that has been widely seen in classrooms for decades is the Simple View of Reading (Gough & Turner, 1986). This model describes reading comprehension as the product of word recognition and language comprehension. The Simple View of Reading (SVR) is widely popular because it highlights the need for both word reading and thinking about the meaning of the language.

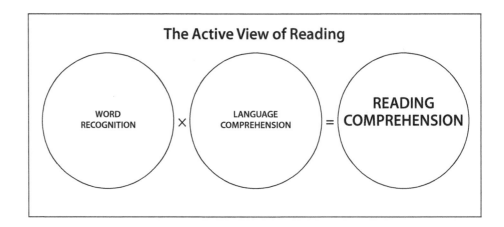

Duke and Cartwright (2021) proposed an adaptation of the Simple View of Reading (SVR, Gough & Turner, 1986): instead of describing reading comprehension as the product of decoding and language comprehension, they proposed other variables that affect the reading process. The Active View of Reading (AVR) introduces more cognitive skills that are considered more malleable. Specifically, there are four broad areas for AVR: self-regulation, word recognition, bridging processes, and language comprehension. It is important to note that when I use the term *reading* I mean *reading comprehension*.

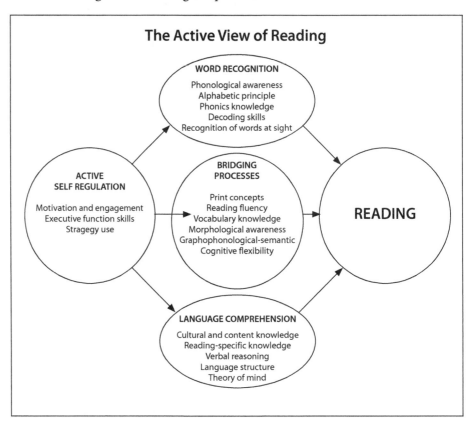

There are three key understandings in the AVR about reading that come from scientific research underscoring some of the complexities of reading that aren't addressed by SVR.

These understandings:

1. point to causes of reading difficulties within and beyond word recognition and language comprehension;
2. reflect the considerable overlap between word recognition and language comprehension and the important processes that bridge these skills and/or operate through that overlap;
3. and represent the important role that active self-regulation plays in reading (Duke & Cartwright, 2021, p. 26).

The AVR model reflects these advanced understandings and this book makes practical connections between each component of the model and classroom instruction. The model is important because it gives teachers avenues to explore and intentional instruction when students have reading difficulties that may not be obvious using old paradigms. It is important for teachers to be able to assess to determine strengths and stretches and target instruction based on the information acquired through assessment.

Building knowledge is the ultimate purpose of reading. Knowledge, which involves information in long-term memory, predicts reading ability and goes beyond just knowing words to knowledge of concepts (Duke & Cartwright, 2021). Humans build knowledge of the natural and social world around them as they interact with texts throughout their lives. The kind of knowledge known will be affected by cultural environments, which sometimes changes assessments on reading and should be considered when evaluating reading abilities. It is important to develop readers who can not only comprehend at a surface level, but at a deep level where transformational thinking may (and often does) occur.

Students gain knowledge from their experiences, which means that each student comes to us with their unique funds of knowledge. Funds of knowledge refers to knowledge acquired from and based on cultural practices that are part of being a family and community and taking part in experiences, as well as daily life. Students' knowledge will differ based on their culture, what they have been exposed to, and their environment, to name just some factors.

A few years ago I overhauled my library to see if the high number of Indigenous students I worked with were being represented in the books I had. I decided to do some research and invest in many local Indigenous books that were recommended by a provincial educational organization called First Nations Education Steering Committee (FNESC) www.fnesc.ca.

In such books my students started to see their culture represented and discussed in more intentional ways. There were vocabulary words and phrases that were familiar to many students (e.g., elders, bannock, Mother Earth, Turtle Island). In addition, there were more discussions about themes students were familiar with that developed from the books, such as the importance of ancestors, environmental stewardship, and life and season cycles. Overall, the students showed more interest in reading books and having discussions about their reading.

The AVR model highlights the importance of cultural knowledge as part of the way we understand language around us. The words we choose and the topics we focus on matter to our students. Our students can see if they are being represented in the books we read and the discussions we facilitate. And if so, then they know that the unique funds of knowledge they bring to our classroom community are valued. According to Duke and Cartwright (2021),

Humans build knowledge of the natural and social world around them as they interact with texts throughout their lives.

This in turn opens the door for considering how and why race, religious background, socioeconomic status, and other factors impact the reading process — why social justice concerns are relevant, even in understanding the process of reading. For example, readers who are rarely provided with opportunities to read texts that reflect their cultural background will experience the reading process differently than those with the privilege of a frequent match of their cultural background and the knowledge assumed by an author/text [p. 37–38].

The Importance of Bridging Processes

In the Simple View of Reading model, word recognition and language comprehension are shown as separate, without impacting each other. In the AVR model, Duke and Cartwright depicted research that shows considerable overlap between word recognition and language comprehension which they call bridging processes. Bridging processes are important for teachers because they show that we do not need to only teach word recognition and language comprehension, but we can also teach across them. By teaching print concepts, reading fluency, vocabulary knowledge, morphological awareness, and graphological-semantic cognitive flexibility, we can strengthen skills in both word recognition and language comprehension by teaching strategies that build skillful readers.

In a grade 2 classroom, I was teaching students about vocabulary development and how many of our picture books have extended vocabulary, even more so than some beginning chapter books (Cruz, 2019). This was an important aspect I wanted them to understand because many students voiced the opinion that reading chapter books was the *real* act of reading. This was problematic for my students who did not have the skills to read chapter books yet and therefore felt like they were not "real" readers. I introduced the class to the book *The Stack,* written by Vanessa Roeder. This is a perfect book for emphasizing vocabulary and fluency because it is written in rhyming form which helps children hear the sing-song aspect of reading with prosody (when to emphasize words and phrase words that make sense together). The author uses sophisticated language within a short amount of text that gives the students context about word meaning through picture clues and the development of the story. For example, on one page you will find the words, "Her quest seemed insurmountable. She had to think much bigger. She planned a complicated scheme to execute with vigor." It is the kind of book that you can read over and over again and notice new aspects to the writing or illustrations with each new reading. The more we read, the more students started to notice how to read the book with expression and phrasing, and the more they asked questions and made inferences about word meanings. The students gained knowledge of word recognition and language comprehension through the focus on vocabulary and fluency.

Active Self-Regulation

Another important addition highlighted in the key understandings that needs to be given some attention is the **active** part of the AVR model. Students are not passive recipients of reading instruction, nor passive readers. There is a lot going on in our brains when we are reading and students are using and building many skills simultaneously and independently. Students are at the centre of reading; they are bringing all the components of reading together to make meaning of text.

Active self-regulation is essentially knowing how to learn and continuing to learn throughout one's life. Our students need to be able to control their thoughts and actions to achieve their reading goals. According to Butler, Schnellert, and Perry (2017), "individuals can take and feel in control over their learning and success if they deliberately and reflectively self-regulate their engagement in activities" (p. 3). We can help our students take control over their engagement in reading so they feel empowered. Skilled readers are active, strategic, and engaged in their reading. Many of the activities in this book are designed to invite students to think deeply about their reading and build a powerful reading identity. The main processes of active self-regulation described in this book are motivation and engagement, executive function skills, and strategy use. These processes will be described in more detail in the next chapter.

A practical example of active self-regulation involves introducing students to designing and creating hands-on science experiments. This activity provides students with individual choice and a concrete reason to learn more about their topic. To increase students' motivation to read, we want them to read because they want to, not because they have to. The students need to do a lot of talking with peers about their ideas for the science experiment, they need to source out information about their topic, and they need to develop a plan.

Active self-regulation is essentially knowing how to learn and continuing to learn throughout one's life.

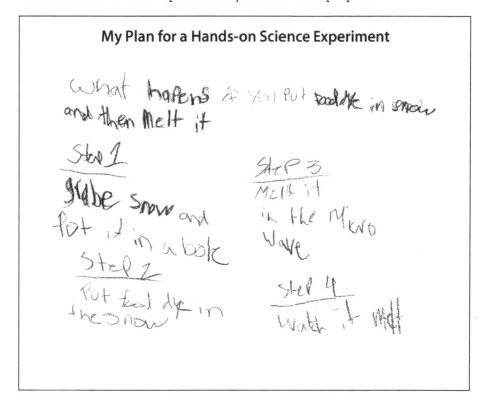

My Plan for a Hands-on Science Experiment

What happens if you put food dye in snow and then melt it

Step 1
grabe snow and put it in a book

Step 2
Put food dye in the snow

Step 3
Melt it in the micro wave

Step 4
Watch it melt

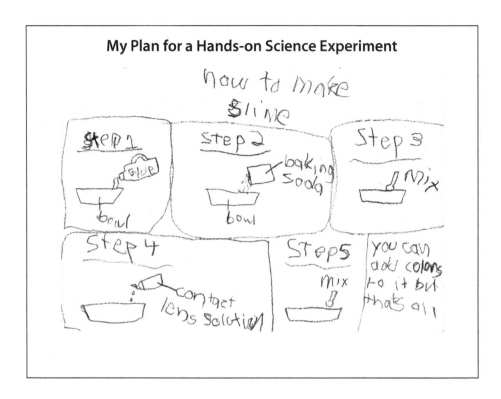

My Plan for a Hands-on Science Experiment

how to make Slime

Step 1 — glue — bowl
Step 2 — baking soda — bowl
Step 3 — mix
Step 4 — contact lens solution
Step 5 — mix — you can add colors to it but that's all

Engagement may look like active participation and attentiveness, as well as the willingness to describe one's own thoughts and ideas while listening to others' thoughts and ideas. Aukerman and Schuldt (2021) describe literate engagement as "the quality and depth of readers' participation with text as they take part in reading and related activities" (p. 89).

The Components of the AVR

There are many different components within the four main categories of active self-regulation, word recognition, language comprehension, and the bridging processes.

Active Self-Regulation

Motivation and Engagement
Reading motivation involves having the desire to read. Motivation facilitates engagement and leads to the active participation in the process of reading and the interaction with text.

Executive Function Skills
This is the ability to set and stay focused on goals when engaging in complex tasks.

Strategy Use
This involves intentional actions that students take to accomplish a specific goal or task that is not yet automatic.

Word Recognition

Phonological Awareness
The ability to recognize and manipulate the spoken parts of words and sentences.

Alphabetic Principle
The knowledge that sounds in spoken language are represented by letters in writing.

Phonics Knowledge
The letter-sound relationship in printed words.

Decoding Skills
The knowledge of sound-letter relationships and the ability to blend those to produce words.

Recognition of Words at Sight
The ability to read a word automatically.

Language Comprehension

Cultural and Other Content Knowledge
Information acquired over time through experiences.

Reading-Specific Background Knowledge
Understanding different aspects of writing, such as how to use text features.

Verbal Reasoning
Making sense of writing through the nuanced part of text such as inferences and interpretations.

Language Structure
The organization of writing to convey meaning, such as sentence structure.

Theory of Mind
Social understanding of how thoughts and feelings of characters impact their behaviors and actions.

Bridging Processes

Print Concepts
Navigating a book and understanding how print works.

Reading Fluency
Reading with accuracy and prosody (expression and phrasing).

Vocabulary Knowledge
Understanding the meaning of words and phrases.

Morphological Awareness
Knowledge and understanding of the smallest meaningful units within words, such as base words, prefixes, and suffixes.

Graphophonological-Semantic Cognitive Flexibility
Actively switching between letter sounds and meaning in print.

This book is set up to highlight different components of the Active View of Reading and describe how this model can look in your classroom. I intentionally have not suggested a program or a specific set of materials to follow because we know it is the teachers and how they teach that make a difference in our students' reading ability. Teaching is not just knowledge about how to execute a good lesson; it involves so many decisions about how much time to spend teaching a skill, which students need further instruction, and what students need to move forward, based on professional judgement. Teachers do not just deliver content; we teach the students who are in front of us and they change from year to year.

Teaching reading is complex and there is no one way to teach the diverse students we have in our classrooms.

2

Active Self-Regulation

Self-regulation is a process. It is not something students simply do or don't acquire. The process is developed day after day as students experience new learning situations that have a level of complexity they want or need to engage with. As teachers, we can support, encourage, and demonstrate approaches to self-regulation, but it is the individual student who needs to actively regulate themselves. We do not have the ability to manage a student's engagement. As adults, we self-regulate daily. Whenever we take on a new learning situation, personal or professional, we are responsible for controlling our engagement. Since self-regulation is a long-long process, it seems necessary to work with students on how they can develop self-regulating skills, even in our youngest learners. Self-regulation is important to the AVR model because it puts students in the active role of navigating their reading rather than being passive responders in their reading process.

Motivation and Engagement

We do not want just compliance, we want engagement from our students.

Motivation drives engagement. It is difficult to be engaged with reading a book if we are not interested in the topic, concept, or storyline. When students encounter challenges, that is when motivation is going to boost their willingness to problem-solve or use strategic action to continue the task and meet their reading goals. Our students need to develop the important components and skills in reading to be proficient, but they also need to develop identities as readers and the desire to want to read. According to Young, Paige, and Rasinski (2022), "students who are read to generally have a better attitude toward reading than students who are not read to" (p. 77).

Elementary classrooms are places where students are not only cognitively engaged but are engaged within a classroom community of learners. Students should be meaningfully engaged in content and in community, not just complying. Such classrooms are places where students are disagreeing with each other, helping peers seek out evidence, constantly questioning, engaging with different perspectives, and socially, emotionally healthy.

Active reading classrooms are also places where students learn with and from each other and where there is a lot of talk time. I was recently asked to design a classroom with an early literacy focus. I immediately brought up the importance of having students reading and writing every day and talking about reading and writing every day. The motivation to read and write would be driven by the motivation to be an active member of a community of learners. The classroom should be a place where students write about what is important to them, in whatever form of writing development that entails. A place where students choose books to read because they are interesting, funny, sad, heartwarming, and all of those emotions together. Classrooms are a place where student's individual and collective thinking is honored and encouraged on a daily basis.

When students are not engaged in reading and writing, perhaps for many different reasons highlighted in the AVR, they may be missing out on the social aspect of engaging with others around text and writing. When children are just word-calling text, they cannot get to the whole interaction with the text because they are not constantly considering what the text means to them and what thinking is being developed in their minds. Word callers can sometimes answer basic comprehension questions about the text; however, they often have difficulty describing their thinking throughout the reading of the text and how the text allowed them to connect with meaning outside the words on the page to the broader message or understanding. Speaking, listening, and having dialogue are critical for building knowledge.

"Certainly much that children read in classrooms is never sculpted and shaped, discussed and written about. Much of what we read passes through the lenses of our eyes to our brains, is comprehended superficially, and never considered again. However, as teachers we need to make sure children have the cognitive ability to consider what is worth savouring, what portion of a text has the potential to change a life, what merits discussion, and what should be lingered over, argued about, and anchored in memory, because to comprehend only literally would be too great a loss" (Keene & Zimmerman, 2007, p. 166).

Classroom Activities for Motivation and Engagement

Read, read, read

To get proficient at most activities we need to have lots of experience doing it. Reading comprehension is no different. The more we read, and read widely, the more we learn to comprehend different kinds of texts.

We can involve our students in guided practice in reading through shared reading, read-alouds, and many other formats of reading with and to students. But students will gain more independence with the act of reading by actively taking part in it through individual reading.

Scoggin and Schneewind (2021) describe the necessities for setting up impactful independent reading by focusing on time, choice, talk, and teacher support.

- Time to read means more time with students' eyes on text. It is important to build up students' stamina for reading in longer chunks of time so students can get into a place of 'flow' with the text. Students can transfer previously learned skills and strategies and play around with them as they build their reading repertoire.

- Giving students choice is a very important way to engage them in the content, style, and interests represented in texts. Students can choose texts that they want to explore, gain knowledge from, and expand their identities as readers.
- Talk is not only important because it develops oral language skills. In terms of reading comprehension, talk assists in the social aspect of developing comprehension through listening to others' ideas and thoughts, and working to develop their own understanding of the text.
- Students will not necessarily develop engagement with text by simply having time to read independently. It involves teacher's support in building stamina, teaching targeted skills and strategies 'just in time' to support where students are in their learning journey. "Joyful independent reading does not happen by accident; it is a conscious collaboration between teachers and students" (p. 4).

Most grade 4 students have had a couple of years of independent reading time at this point of their learning journey. Some students love it, and some students try everything to avoid it. With one particular class, I wanted students to understand the benefits of being engaged during independent reading so they could reap the benefits (academic, social, emotional, and self-regulatory), and I could focus on the important work of teaching targeted skills and strategies.

I decided I would use the power of peer interaction. I asked the students to think about themselves as readers. I asked them to share a time when they were really interested in a book they were reading. I asked them to turn and talk with a peer, and then we shared experiences with the whole group. Some students gave me examples such as, "When I was reading a series, I couldn't wait to see what the characters would do in the next book", "I couldn't believe what I learned about living in the Roman Empire and that made me want to learn more", and "the book I was reading reminded me of visiting my grandma on the farm." I explained those were interesting things to share with others. So interesting we were going to make an anchor chart of what it feels like when we are engaged in reading.

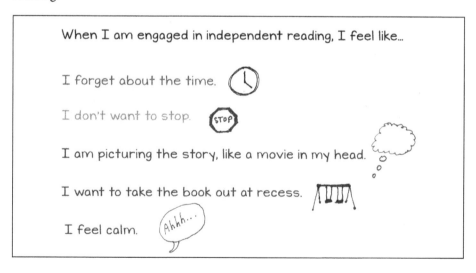

The anchor chart allowed students to check in with themselves as they were reading and notice how they were feeling. By listening to how engaged their peers were with independent reading, my reluctant readers started to understand the appeal of what their classmates were gaining from this time in the classroom.

Writing about Reading

Invite students to continue their engagement with text by writing about it. A powerful activity involves having students write down their thoughts about character development, how their thinking changed throughout a story, what surprised them, what made them feel emotion, and how they can translate all that thinking into their own narrative or informational writing. Writing about reading allows students to continue the journey through exploring their own ideas and thoughts, as well as creating new aspects of story they may not have imagined without the support of the text.

For example, a strategy I use to get my students thinking about how a character has changed throughout a story is to have them write what they think the character might be thinking. I decide ahead of time where I am going to stop and have my students do some writing. In the book *Giraffes Can't Dance* by Giles Andreae, I chose three pages for my students to think about how Gerald the giraffe is feeling and what his internal thoughts might be at those moments. I give them a thought bubble graphic organizer to complete as we are reading the book and then add illustrations or more writing when the story is finished.

Writing about reading extends students' learning beyond the text and continues the learning after finishing reading.

(see template, pg 105)

Writing about reading can also be a bridge across content areas to reinforce engagement in text through learning about science or social studies. Students can organize their knowledge on a topic or concept through considering what they knew before they read the text, how their thinking changed, and what new information they have to add to their existing knowledge.

Teach a Friend

Imagine the motivation and engagement when students are told, "I'm going to teach you something and then you are going to get the chance to teach a friend." Students will often listen very closely and internalize information if they know they will be mentoring in the place of the teacher in front of peers.

When I was teaching grade 1 students how to use a table of contents in a non-fiction information book, I explained that this is a guide that is helpful to see what information they will find in the book. With one half of the class, I practiced looking at the table of contents and coming up with information that we would learn in that section, as well as what questions were already forming in our brains. I used a National Geographic Kids book called *Penguins!* by Anne Schreiber to model how to use the table of contents, and the students used other National Geographic Kids books about animals when they mentored their peers. We talked at length about the different chapters we could explore and what information we were hoping to find out. The students were thrilled that they could go to specific chapters of interest, rather than having to read the book from front to back. Some students were most interested in chapter 6, "A Chick is Born", while others wanted to learn more about what a Penguin Parade was in chapter 8. Once students had some guided practice, they were off to teach the other half of the class how to effectively use the table of contents. I heard comments like, "This will help you with your reading," and, "You don't have to read the book in order like other books, you can go to the section you are most interested in learning." I also heard the mentoring students prompting other students by asking, "What

To teach someone something is to understand it in depth.

questions do you have about this section?" and "what vocabulary words do you expect to see in this section?"

Read Aloud for Pleasure

When teaching grade 3 students, I decided to engage them in the sense of story by reading *A Series of Unfortunate Events,* a series of stories by Lemony Snicket. I chose to read for twenty minutes each day while my students were eating lunch. By the second book in the series, my students were hooked. Lunchtime became a quiet time for students to look forward to listening to a fluent adult read aloud from a book they were interested in and excited to hear. I would casually introduce literary techniques, such as foreshadowing and cliffhangers, and discuss aspects of character development through the continuous journey of three orphan children. There were no formal expectations for students to do any writing, analyzing, or discussing of the books; all they had to do was enjoy listening to the story. However, many students chose to emulate the writing style of Lemony Snicket in their own story-writing, they had discussions on the playground about their predictions of the story, and some students found other books in the series in the library and read ahead to find out what was going to happen before the rest of the class. By using twenty minutes each day to connect with the students through the reading of the series, I was able to impact many different areas of literacy.

Selling Books

When working with a class of grade 6 students, I wanted to find a way to hook the reluctant readers during independent reading time. These were the students who did a lot of 'pretend reading.' I started to sell books. I would choose one book each day to introduce to the students by saying something like, "If you like to read about natural disasters and what happens to people who live in areas of natural disasters, you would probably love this book called *The Wave,* by Eric Walters. I will read you the first couple of pages to see if this is a book for you." I would make sure to have two copies of the book, as sometimes students would decide to read the book simultaneously to discuss what was happening. I would 'sell' a variety of genres to meet the interest needs of the students. I would also make sure that I read many of the books I was selling so that I could have discussions with students about their books to engage them further and create a sense of common interests. Sometimes I would have students sell their books to their classmates. This invitation would work when students were encouraged to continue reading so that they could discuss the book with peers. I overheard one student say to another, "Did you get to the part where they started to climb the mountain and had to stay there all night because they were trapped? What do you think of the main character?"

The following two student responses are from the book *The Quiltmaker's Gift,* by Jeff Brumbeau and Gail de Marcken. The book is about a quiltmaker who makes beautiful quilts and gives them away.

We can use our students to promote reading to their peers. It is much more powerful than using just our opinions.

The quilt makers gift

This is a book about a quilt maker who's very good at making quilts. Then a greedy king made the people celebrate his birthday twice a year. He had a bunch of nice things. This king wasn't happy with the gifts. The lady wouldn't let the king have her quilt. She was brought to a bear cave where she made friends with the bear. The quilt maker endured all that the king did. Eventually the king realized and started giving his things away. Then the quilt maker gave him a quilt in return.

the quilt makers gift

in the town theres a king who loves gifts but never gives them only recieves them from people in the town. he made it so everyone has to give him a gift on his two birthdays and christmas but theres a woman who lives in the mountain who makes quilts but only for poor people. the king finds out and demandes he gives her one. she said she would only give him one if he gives away all his

presents. but he doesnt wantcto to that. so he puts her in places where its dangerous but she still refuse so he gives up and gives away his presents till hes left with nothing. then the quilt maker finds him and gives him his quilt and he is then finally happy.

Quick and Easy Strategies to Encourage Engagement

- Co-create strategies on an anchor chart that can be added to throughout the year as students come up with ways to check engagement. Some ideas might be to grab a stress tool to focus the mind while focusing the body, or draw circles on a scrap piece of paper. Our youngest learners can be taught to gently massage their arm or hand to be more present for learning.

- Movement is always a great way to give our brains a boost of energy and focus. Brain and body breaks can involve simple stretches, partner walks, yoga poses, or even jumping jacks. The whole class has some time to move, release some energy, and refocus.

- When students are engaging in a listening activity such as a mini-lesson, a good rule of thumb is that they can generally focus for the number of minutes that equals their age. So, if you have a class of six-year-olds, they will generally be able to focus their attention for six minutes before needing a break.

- There are many important reasons to give students choices, but a huge one is the increase in motivation. Two or three choices is enough. If we give more choices, we risk overwhelming our students and they may focus more on the choice they have to make than on the learning. A choice can be as simple as, "Would you like to write on paper or your white board?" Or, "Would you like to sit or stand while I give directions for the next activity?" Giving students a choice to make immediately engages them because it puts them in control of an aspect of their learning.

- A quick check-in with students can help them identify how they are feeling about their engagement or about their learning. You can do a quick check-in for understanding by having students give you a thumbs up, thumbs down, or thumbs sideways to represent "I understand, I don't understand, I kind of understand." Another check-in strategy is to have students rate their energy/focus on a scale of 1 to 5. Students can let you know how they are feeling by holding up the corresponding number of fingers. Check-ins are helpful for teachers to see how students are feeling, but even more than that they are helpful for students to reflect and identify how they are feeling and what they need to adjust to continue their learning.

- Co-create a mental model of what it feels like when you are engaged in learning. Have students describe what it feels like in their bodies, in their minds, and in their environment when they are focused on and interested in learning. They may say, "My heart is not beating really fast, I feel like my brain wants to learn more, or I am able to take deep breaths." You can make an anchor chart to refer to throughout the year so students can monitor their engagement.

- Many of our students may not come to school having an emotional vocabulary beyond words like *happy* and *sad*. It is important for students to describe how they are feeling because that will engage them to notice their state and then develop strategies to adjust if needed. I've had students say to me in the past, "My brain feels tired," and "My legs feel like they are shaking." Those are really great descriptions of students who need a break in order for them to engage in learning. Some good vocabulary words are *excited, anxious, distracted, motivated*, and *exhausted*.

- An important part of motivation and engagement is having a growth mindset (Dweck, 2006). A growth mindset is having the belief that you will accomplish goals through effort and persistence. It would be very difficult for our students to keep a level of engagement in an activity if they felt discouraged. Students with a fixed mindset feel like they can either accomplish a goal or not. These students may feel that there is no point continuing an activity once they hit an obstacle to their learning or some sort of challenge. Teachers can teach students the difference between growth and fixed mindsets so they have the language to describe their learning beliefs.

Executive Function Skills

Executive functioning (EF) skills are mental skills that help us manage complex tasks such as planning, organization, monitoring, and strategy use, which are more complex than the three core skills that underlie them: working memory, cognitive flexibility, and self-control. EF skills are at the centre of goal-directed, active self-regulation. EF skills are essentially students' control over their own thinking.

Planning is important as it requires setting and deciding how to work towards a goal. It is intentional and purposeful. Organizing requires putting tasks in order to accomplish a goal.

In terms of reading, usually the goal when approaching text is to understand it. Readers approach a text with a goal in mind before even beginning the process of reading. Organizing how to comprehend the text can be as simple as students asking themselves questions before, during, and after reading. So, in this example, organization supports planning because it allows students to execute their plan.

Planning and organizing look different depending on the choice of text. In a narrative text, such as *Giraffes Can't Dance*, by Giles Andreae, students may already be intrigued by the title and cover of the book. The book is about Gerald, a giraffe that wants nothing more than to be able to dance at the annual Jungle Dance. Unfortunately, he is less than coordinated and all the other animals laugh at him. It takes the wise words of a cricket to encourage him to find his inner song and let the sounds move him. The other animals are amazed at the new ways he can move his body and Gerald's self-confidence increases. As students look at the cover of the book and the title, they can set themselves up for an interesting book in which the animals act like people and speak like people. That is quite different from planning and organizing to read the book, *Facts about the Beaver: A Picture Book for Kids*, by Lisa Strattin. To get ready to read this informational book, readers are already thinking about what they know about beavers, what they are hoping to learn about beavers, and what vocabulary words they may encounter. Each of these examples set students up to consider their goal of understanding the text.

Let's examine the three core skills that underlie the more complex skills of planning and organizing: working memory, cognitive flexibility, and self-control.

Working Memory

Working memory allows students to hold important information in their heads to use part of the information at a given time. It allows students to hold strings of sounds as they decode, hold meaning as they are reading, and adapt and change their thoughts as new information is learned. When students begin to learn how to read, they are practicing keeping information in their working memory while they are reading. It is helpful for children to hear books read to them from an early age (birth) for many reasons, but one important one is so that they can start to strengthen their working memory and hold storylines in their heads.

A grade 2 student who I was working with on reading intervention knew many strategies to try out when she came to a word she didn't know. She could tell me about her strategies and explain how she solved unknown words. However, as soon as she began reading again after word-solving, she forgot what the story was about. We had to stop and discuss the story and then she was able to continue. I realized that she might be having difficulties with her working memory, as it was not developed enough for her to hold onto the story when she left it momentarily. She was not able to build and hold onto the overall text meaning. We needed to build up her working memory in order to build up her reading comprehension; otherwise, all the strategies in her back pocket were not going to help her become a proficient reader.

Once I realized the potential issue, I was able to help her by creating some strategies that helped her focus in on key concepts that would eventually jog her memory about the text. For example, at the end of each page we would come up with a word or phrase that described what was happening in the text and I would write it on a sticky note that we kept beside her. When we finished the next page, we would go through the same action. We worked on this strategy for at least a week before I started to hold back and let her come up with the word or phrase by herself and write it by herself. The act of reflecting on what she had just read helped her keep smaller chunks of information at her fingertips to rely on if she needed to use her cognitive ability to problem solve at the word level.

Cognitive Flexibility

Cognitive flexibility is apparent when students hold multiple parts of a task in their mind and switch back and forth between them as needed. In terms of reading, cognitive flexibility allows students to decode words alongside making meaning of text.

A common reading difficulty among students I've worked with, especially in late primary grades, is the lack of monitoring while they are reading. At some point in their reading journey, they may have developed the misguided notion that reading is decoding and not thinking about meaning, or perhaps they lacked the ability to decode and make meaning at the same time. These students could read (decode) entire pages without realizing that what they were saying out loud did not make sense. Generally, self-correcting while reading involves saying a word or phrase, realizing it does not make sense, and going back to do some word-solving to ensure it does make sense. The students who were only decoding, or word calling, were not self-correcting as they read. Sometimes they said nonsense words and did not realize they were not English words, until we discussed it.

Self-Control

Self-control is also referred to as inhibitory control or impulse control.

Self-control is a skill that both allows students to ignore irrelevant information and suppresses responses that could detract from the task at hand. Self-control is evident in many cognitive activities that students engage in, and it is definitely very important when reading in order for students to get to a place of deep comprehension.

Consider your own reading of text.

- Have you ever read the same page three times because you were getting distracted and lacked the self-control needed to ignore external stimuli?
- Have you ever read a difficult text and realized you focused so much on trying to figure out what words meant by using context clues that you didn't remember what the overall text was about?
- Have you ever had a conversation about a book and realized that you completely missed the nuanced information within the text?

Cartwright (2023) explains, "Skilled reading is remarkably complex and requires readers to juggle actively multiple sources of information in text, integrate that information with what we already know, and consciously monitor their own understanding to produce nuanced interpretations of text content. In short, reading is thinking, very active and incredibly complex thinking" (p. 11). Therefore, executive function skills help students become managers of their own brains, pulling up information when it is needed and keeping things on track. Coordination of skills is required between word reading and language comprehension as those components work together as students learn to read.

Executive Function Skills in Action

EF skills do not happen in isolation, they are connected and happening all at the same time. Let's consider how EF skills help us when we go on a trip to the grocery store.

We use executive function skills every day.

Planning: to prepare to go to the grocery store, the planning often happens before even leaving the house. I list what I need as I make decisions about recipes I'm planning to make. And I will often check on the 'staple food items' to see what they are running low on to add to the list.

Organization: as the list is being created, shoppers may choose to put items together on the list that can be found in the same department (produce, dairy, meat, etc.). When shopping people usually need to constantly refer to the list to ensure they are not forgetting anything.

Cognitive flexibility: grocery shoppers need to be looking for items on their list, greeting people they know, thinking about the recipes they are planning to make and whether they need to be adapted based on the items that are available.

Working memory: shoppers need to hold the grocery list (somewhat) in their mind while focusing on choosing brands of products and comparing quality and prices of items.

Self-control: the difficult part of grocery shopping when there are so many choices is not getting distracted by considering products that are not on the list or overwhelmed by the amount of choice of the same product. How many different kinds of peanut butter can there be?

That is a lot of active thinking going on in a simple task of grocery shopping. Now let's consider the complex task of reading.

Before Reading a Text

Students are already thinking as they consider the cover of a book, the title, and even perhaps the author. They are asking themselves, What do I already know about this topic? What am I going to pay attention to in this text? What are my predictions about the information or storyline I may encounter in this text? These planning questions represent how active our students are as they get ready to read. At this point, students' curiosity is building and that is getting them primed for learning new information. Planning to approach text is very similar to planning to approach a task such as students might encounter in problem-based learning, which is a way to emphasize to students that reading is an active task.

As proficient readers, we also plan as we get ready to read. If I picked up an advanced carpentry text knowing that I have very limited background knowledge of woodworking, I would make some decisions about reading behaviors. I would plan on paying close attention to text features that would help me understand it (diagrams, captions, photos, subtitles). I would also have my search engine open on my computer in case I needed to quickly look up a word or a concept through a written description or perhaps a YouTube video. I would also plan on going very slowly with my goal being deep understanding rather than speed at reading the text.

Our students can be taught to approach their text in a similar way. I was recently in a kindergarten classroom where students were getting ready to write in their book-making time. Students were given blank pieces of paper stapled together to replicate a book. One girl came up to me and said, "When I get started to write but I'm not sure which side to start on, I go to our bookshelf and open those books so I can start my book the same way." That girl showed very intentional planning skills that set her up to meet the goal she set for herself about writing in her book on the correct pages.

Teachers can support students' ability to practice planning with a few key instructional practices:

- Describe a planning strategy and explain why readers use it.
- Model questioning when reading real books with or to students by asking, "Why am I reading this book?"
- Plan together during a shared reading experience.
- Intentionally set up planning time when conferencing with individuals or small groups.

Before my grade 2 students and I began to do a shared reading of the book *Be a Good Ancestor* by Leona Prince and Gabrielle Prince, I had my students jot down some thoughts, ideas, and questions they had about the book by looking at the cover, the title, and the authors. I wanted students to get their reading brains ready and start to prepare their thoughts about the story.

Asher

It coud be a fiction book
because it dosn't seem reel.
And the bird itsnt reel. And
the lady look fake like
she can FLY.

I think the Main chatter
is A Mom and A k.d
and a bird

I would expect to find
out that the ancestor is
good

that the mom is talling
the kid and shes beeing
good

Its a non fiction becaus
its true

Be a good Ansestor

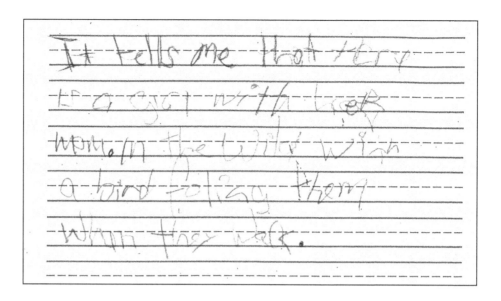

It tells me that they
lf a eyet with tree
worm in the tilt with
a bird foliag they
whun they wet.

While Reading a Text

Students are thinking about the meaning of text and constantly asking themselves questions as they search for information. As students predict meaning of text or what may happen next in text, they are using cognitive flexibility to consider information and then change thinking based on new information. Students are using their working memory to hold information and consider what is not directly in the text by inferring. In fiction, they may also be considering characters' internal motives to try and figure out reasons the characters act in certain ways in order to get a deep understanding of the text. Depending on a student's reading ability, they may be doing all this complex thinking at the same time as decoding and using what they know about phonics to solve unknown words.

In terms of organization when reading, our brains are already designed to look for patterns and notice similarities in information. This generally occurs before students begin the task of reading and continues into the act of reading. Without some sense of organization, it is difficult to manage other EF skills. Organization is evident in our English language through words, structures, and types of texts. Students can use what they know about organization to help them understand the text through story retellings, sound-spelling patterns, making connections to prior knowledge, and the use of text features.

While reading the book *Be a Good Ancestor,* my students began to rely on the way the book was written to make sense of the content. The book is about the cyclical nature of the world around us and how all living things are connected in various ways. The writing on one page reads:

> Be a good ancestor with the land.
> Seeds become seedlings.
> Seedlings become trees.
> Trees become forests.
> Forests become oxygen.

My students quickly decided they would do some work on sketching the cycles mentioned in the book to make better sense of the connections. Because all the pages are written in a similar format, the organization of the text helped support understanding the content.

After Reading a Text

Through discussions about the text, students will engage in cognitive flexibility to think and talk about how they are using newly acquired knowledge to connect to previous knowledge or consider information in a new way. They are also practicing self-control when they focus on what was learned from the text.

In the digital age, children's attention is constantly distracted by digital stimuli. Maryanne Wolfe (2018) worries that children are slowly losing their developmental capacity to draw analogies and inferences when reading text. Reading is becoming a scan of words to get an overview of general information, rather than deep reading to gain fuller knowledge, assess the information based on background knowledge, and build new theories about a topic. What people read and how people read change how they think.

EF can be strengthened in the classroom in task-specific ways.

- Students can create and rely on lists as a concrete method of managing complex tasks.
- Slow down instruction so students have lots of time to process.
- Offer external supports until they become internal (e.g., individual anchor charts connected to their goals).
- Teach reading strategies that will help students remember what they have read (read one page and then sketch a picture related to the substance of the text, increase to read two pages and then sketch what is happening).
- Check out *Sesame Street*'s "Guess What Is Next" pattern development for support practicing and building pattern recognition.

We can help our students develop an active view of reading by supporting them in building a reading life. Invite your students to understand that their brains are changing by noticing, naming, and nurturing when we are practicing using strategies. You can include students in decision making to increase their independence and create a sense of a community of readers. Explain and emphasize that the main goal of reading is to build knowledge by using the language that students can replicate and then use in their own vocabulary.

Setting Goals

Goal setting requires students to make a plan to understand the text which utilizes EF skills as they establish their plan, monitor it, and use strategies to stick to it. Goal setting creates independence and helps to maintain engagement while reading.

Ask students, "What do you want to learn or gain from this text?" Setting goals is an important part of getting our brains ready to experience a learning activity when we are reading. Setting goals allows students to take charge of their own learning and realize that they need to be active participants in the learning, to get out of it what they want to. By giving students a sense of ownership, we encourage them to be more committed to the learning process and therefore more engaged.

If students are about to read:

- a non-fiction text, ask, "What do you already know about this content or topic?" or "What vocabulary words or key concepts do you expect to see in this book?"

Ask students, "What do you want to learn or gain from this text?"

- a book in a series, ask, "What do you already know about the lead character [e.g., Nate the Great]?"
- a work by a familiar author, ask, "What do we know about the author's [e.g., Jacqueline Woodson's] writing?"

Strategy Use

Strategies are practical processes that are mindful, which means that people must be paying attention when using them. Strategies differ from skills because skills require automatic use of the skills themselves while strategies are conscious. Students can practice the strategies repeatedly until they become skills with automaticity. When students become more automatic in their use of strategies, they can pay attention to other important things such as remembering what they are reading.

The action of using strategies often includes the following steps:

1. understanding the task and setting goals;
2. planning;
3. enacting strategies;
4. monitoring;
5. adjusting (Butler et al., 2011).

That looks like a lot of steps considering we use strategies all the time, but the steps often happen very quickly when we are reading. For example, if a student is reading a book and comes to a word they don't know, they quickly understand that some sort of action is needed to figure out the word. They may think of strategies they have used in the past to solve words and decide which one to try first. The student then monitors by considering if the strategy worked (e.g., does the word make sense in this context?). If the answer is no, the student can adjust and try a different strategy.

Effectively using strategic action when reading involves students using executive functioning skills to hold onto the meaning of the text while they problem-solve; otherwise, they will lose the meaning of the text.

In this chapter we discussed a significant part of the AVR model that differs from the SVR and many other models of reading comprehension. Duke and Cartwright (2021) researched the importance of putting students at the centre of their learning by creating active self-regulation as a process of putting students in an active role when navigating their reading. Motivation and engagement are critical to reading. As teachers, we cannot force our students to be motivated and engaged in their reading, but we can set up routines and structures that encourage motivation and engagement. Executive functioning skills are another area in which students can be active in their reading journey. Overarching complex EF skills such as planning, organization, monitoring, and using specific strategies are essential to consider as we work with students with differentiated skill sets.

In the next chapter, we will continue to unpack the AVR model by focusing in on the word recognition component. This chapter will be important for all elementary teachers to understand, as many of our students are at different parts of their learning journey in all elementary grades; however, it will be even more beneficial for teachers teaching in the primary grades. We will explore how word recognition is built through phonological awareness, the alphabetic principle, phonics knowledge, decoding skills, and recognition of words at sight.

3

Word Recognition

Word recognition closely interacts with language comprehension. Word recognition can be described as the ability to recognize words and spelling patterns. The skills associated with word recognition develop over time through many different experiences with connected texts, with sounds in words, and with individual words. It is built by understanding sounds and letters in language. A skilled reader is able to know a word automatically; they don't have to consciously think about it. The funny thing is that you can't tell your brain not to read a word. Try it! Try to look at a word and not read it!

Each of the parts of the Active View of Reading (AVR) are stronger as they develop together. The parts do not develop in isolation. The more students read, the more they recognize words and the more they recognize words, the more they read. Many students can decode but they struggle with automaticity, which means that they are slowed down as they think deeply about words and their meanings. Language comprehension is foundational for word recognition. Students use what they know about language structures to help them with word recognition.

Foundational skills of reading — phonological awareness, phonemic awareness, phonics, print awareness, and concepts of print — are essential to developing the process of reading because they allow for the automaticity of reading words. When children have the foundational skills, they have the gift of time to think deeply about the meaning of the text rather than struggling to decode each word or remember high-frequency words.

Consider the child who is just beginning to read a basic text such as *Gossie & Gertie* by Olivier Dunrea. The story is about two ducks who are best friends and play together. One page reads, "They splash in the rain. They play hide-and-seek in the daisies." When students know some high-frequency words, they can read those words with confidence and competence, which frees up their thinking to consider what an unknown word may mean and how to figure it out. They may consider the storyline, decodable words, the picture aiding the text, and combining all their foundational reading skills with their phonemic and print awareness skills and phonics.

My sister's son was a struggling reader. He did not learn to read until he was in grade 4. He did not see the point in learning to read and was not motivated to develop phonemic awareness, print knowledge, and high-frequency word automaticity. Coming from a family of voracious readers, my sister was stymied. She decided to try encouraging him through the love of story. Every night they would read a few pages of the Harry Potter series by J.K. Rowling. It was a special time for them to interact together and connect through the story of a young wizard. About a year later, his teacher contacted my sister and asked what was happening at home because Brennan was falling asleep in class. It turns out Bren had taught himself to read in order to keep reading after his lights were supposed to be out and he was supposed to be sleeping. The love of story had been the motivation he needed to put all the pieces together and become a voracious reader. Donalyn Miller (2009) might have said that Bren was an "underground reader" because he saw the reading he was doing in school as being completely separate from the reading he preferred to do on his own. Miller states, "underground readers just want to read and for the teacher to get out of the way and let them" (p. 30).

Phonological Awareness (Syllables, Phonemes, Etc.)

Phonological awareness refers to a child's ability to notice and manipulate the parts (phonemes, syllables) in spoken words and sentences. When children are born, they generally begin to learn language informally. At that point in the learning process, children are not concerned about rules and constraints of language. They accumulate and build on prior knowledge and start to make sense of the world around them through communication and language. Upon entering preschool or Kindergarten, children begin to become exposed to other aspects of language, essentially communication through print.

Phonological awareness is an entry point for our youngest students to begin to notice language in ways they haven't explored before. They are taught how to notice, articulate, and manipulate sounds in words. This process is not natural for humans; they need to make new connections in their brains and the language processing system in their brain now has a new job.

Our students need to understand the connection between reading, writing, and oral language. To provide our students with small bursts of explicit instruction, we can weave phonological and phonemic awareness activities throughout the day in meaningful ways.

This is an entry point for our students to notice the similarities and differences in sounds, words, and sentences. Once they are able to recognize those subtle differences, then we want to put them in control of manipulating sounds and words.

Classroom Activities to Support Phonological Awareness

Songs and Nursery Rhymes

A spontaneous and natural invitation for our students to start to notice differences through rhyme, alliteration, syllables, blending, and segmenting sounds is through singing. Introduce songs into whole-class routines so students hear repetitions of the words over and over. Once students have embraced a song as part of their classroom routine, invite students to play around with the lyrics or sounds within words. Students will have more confidence to explore and change words or sounds on their own.

This process is not natural for humans; they need to make new connections in their brains and the language processing system in their brains now have a new job.

For example:

- "Old McDonald Had a Farm" could be changed to "Old McDonald Had a Forest", and the farm animals could become forest animals.

The students will start to play around with lyrics, but then you can explicitly point out other ways to explore the song:

- Let's clap out the syllable of the new word you have introduced [for-est].
- Let's figure out the beginning sound of the new word you have used [squirrel — s].
- Let's come up with a rhyming word for the new word you have used [bear — scare].

Some books that support rhyme awareness are:
Anna Banana — 101 Jump Rope Rhymes by Joanna Cole
Each Peach Pear Plum by Janet and Allan Ahlberg
Father Fox's Pennyrhymes by Clyde and Wendy Watson
Goodnight Moon by Margaret Wise Brown
Is Your Mama a Llama? by Deborah Guarino
The Lady with the Alligator Purse by Mary Ann Hoberman and Nadine Westcott
Mrs. McNosh Hangs Up Her Wash by Sarah Weeks

Simple songs that focus on different skills through an active analysis of sounds are easy to come up with when you have only one minute to practice some phonemic awareness.
For example:

- What is the sound that starts these words: fish, fast, first? F is the sound that starts these words: fish, fast, first.
- What is the sound that ends these words: pot, sat, late? T is the sound that ends these words: pot, sat, late.

Students are thrilled when they get to come up with new words for songs. They can practice as partners, in groups, or on their own.

Poems

Check out Adrienne Gear's book *Powerful Poetry: Read, Write, Rejoice, Recite Poetry All Year Long* for more great ideas.

Introducing poetry is like inviting students to work with songs. Generally, poems are shorter and easier to read and recite at the emerging reader level. You can introduce students to poetry by writing out a poem on a piece of chart paper, white board, or smartboard, but ensure it is place somewhere visible so you can refer to it over and over as students learn new ways to work with the language.

As you read a poem to your students for the first time, you want them to enjoy the lyrical wonder that poetry can offer us. After discussing the poem, the whole class can listen to you read it again and this time you can encourage them to notice your finger pointing to each word, return swipe when you get to the end of the page, and exaggerated stops at periods (to take a breath).
Some books that support learning through poetry are:

Alligator Pie by Dennis Lee
Garbage Delight by Dennis Lee

I Hear You Forest by Kallie George and Carmen Mok
Just around the Corner: Poems about Seasons by Leland B. Jacobs

Clapping Syllables

Clapping out syllables when students say a word slowly helps students notice that words are not only one sound but are actually made up of smaller units of sound. It is beneficial to begin clapping students' names, as their names are very familiar to them and hold a lot of meaning for them. You can engage students in clapping out syllables in names when you are calling out attendance, or when you are having a morning meeting, or even when you are calling students to join you at the carpet. Once students are familiar with the process of clapping syllables in names, you can begin to clap syllables when you are reading a morning message, or when other important words are analyzed in the classroom. Whenever we had a visitor in my Kindergarten classroom, we would learn the visitor's name by clapping out the syllable or syllables in it, writing it on the board, and noticing features of the name. This process made visitors feel special, let my students practice their phonological awareness skills, and increased the students' ability to remember the name of the visitor.

Clapping syllables can naturally and developmentally lead to students putting together and taking apart syllables in words so they have a concrete understanding of how words are made up of more than one sound. Teachers can start with compound words like classroom or leapfrog, because it is easier to hear and discriminate the two parts of such words. You can then move on to two-syllable, simple words, like picnic and swimming. Once students have a good understanding of syllabification, you can move on to multisyllabic words.

Rhyming

Noticing rhymes in words helps teach students to focus their attention on the small units of sounds within words. What is the rhyming part? And what is the part that is different? Students can later transfer rhyme recognition to making word analogies that will empower them to solve unknown words. For example, you can prompt students to solve an unknown word by saying, "You know the word 'sat', can you figure out the word 'chat'? Rhymes come in three levels of difficulty: first knowledge of recognized words, then discrimination, and finally production of an original rhyme. It is far easier for your youngest learners to recognize if two words rhyme than it is to produce rhyming words.

A quick activity that can show you where your class is with their rhyming knowledge is to say two words and have students give you a thumbs up if they rhyme and a thumbs down if they don't rhyme. Immediately you can see where you need to begin your instruction with the whole class, or who needs some small group work on rhyme recognition.

There are many ways to work on rhyming with your students in fun ways that weave throughout the day and take very little effort or preparation to do.

- Categorize pictures of objects and put the pictures together in a line if they rhyme.
- "I spy with my little eye something that rhymes with ___." You can play this as you are waiting for your library time or getting dressed to go outside.
- "Tell me a word — tell me a word that rhymes with hop. Who can think of a different one?"

- Sing "Down by the Bay" with many variations on the original version. Have students come up with rhymes that fit the sentence structure of the song. *Have you ever seen a bear combing his hair? Have you ever seen a mouse trying to get in your house?*
- Students can use handheld mirrors to watch their mouth, tongue, and lips as they say rhyming words to see if their mouths make similar shapes.

Sentence Segmentation

The differences between a letter, a word, and a sentence are quite abstract for our beginning readers. They need explicit teaching about what the differences are as they progress in skills towards phoneme segmenting and blending. A great way to determine a student's knowledge is to sit with a book between you and the student and prompt:

- Point to a word.
- Point to the letter *t*.
- Point to the end of the sentence.
- Point to the beginning of the sentence.

This quick formative assessment is valuable when explicitly teaching print concepts.

A beginning point to begin explicit instruction on sentence segmentation involves blocks. You can have students seated around you at a carpet or at their tables. Tell them they are going to put one block down for every word you say in a sentence. Explain that they need to put the blocks down in a specific way.

Model saying a sentence out loud and have the students clap the number of words with you. Starting at the left-hand side of your table or mat, say the first word and put the first block down to represent it. Then say the second word and make a large finger space before putting down the second block. Continue to follow that format until the end of the sentence. Explain to students that you need to leave a large space between words just as they do in (refer to the title of a big book you have displayed). And I need my blocks to start at this side of my mat and go in this direction, just as the authors do in (display) book.

Start with simple, three- to five-word sentences that only have monosyllabic words.

> My cat is black.
> My house is green.
> Our pet is a cat.
> I play at the park.

Notice which students need more explicit instruction and practice with this skill and if necessary add it into a small group intervention around phonological awareness skills.

Blending and Segmenting Phonemes

Phonemes (sounds in words) are difficult to distinguish because students are used to hearing a word as one sound and thinking about a word as a whole. Also, when we speak, often phoneme sounds overlap one another and make the process of hearing and distinguishing individual sounds in words even more difficult. That is why we play with language in the early years to give students some practice with noticing and manipulating words and sounds. The understanding that words are made up of small units of sound sets up students to successfully decode (read) and encode (write) words.

Blending and segmenting sounds in words is an incredibly important step to reading and writing. When students are working on beginning reading skills, they are noticing the letters in words and blending the sounds together to pronounce the word correctly. When students are beginning to write, they are saying the words they want to print and stretching out the sounds to write them down in the correct order. The processes are reciprocal and as a child learns to blend phonemes it is a natural fit to learn how to segment them as well.

There are many ways that you can incorporate short bursts of instruction and practice throughout the day. A couple of areas to pay attention to are how students are saying the sounds in words when they are segmenting. You will want to teach them early on what the difference is between 'stop sounds' and 'continuous sounds'.

Stop sounds only need a single puff of air (for example, /b/, /p/, /d/, /t/, /k/, /g/). If the students don't learn about how to say them, they may say those letters with a schwa sound (or an "uh" sound) at the end, making all the letters sound like "b-uh", "p-uh", "d-uh", etc. That will be problematic when they start working with letters and want to put "uh" after each stop sound. I found it helpful to show students how they can say those sounds with just one short, quick puff of air. We put our hands in front of our mouths and practice saying those letters and feeling a quick burst of air on our hands.

Continuous sounds can be held until we are out of breath (for example, /f/, /m/, /n/, /s/, /r/).

Sound Walls

Giving students small mirrors to look at their mouths is a helpful support.

Sound walls can help support students learn and extend their knowledge of how sounds work and how they are connected to letters and spelling patterns. Sound walls typically are arranged to show a picture of a student's mouth next to each sound so students can match the way their mouth feels, looks, and acts as they say each sound. By using sound walls, we are utilizing a speech-to-print learning progression. Starting with speech builds on what most students are competent with when they begin their reading journey, and then connects what they know about the spoken language to what they are learning about printed language.

Elkonin Boxes (Sound Boxes)

Elkonin boxes are named after the Russian psychologist who pioneered the method of isolating sounds in words with boxes for our early learners. Putting sounds into boxes as students slowly say words out loud is a concrete way to approach an abstract concept.

(see template, pg 107)

You can model how to use Elkonin boxes with a whole class as you say a word out loud, and involve your students in figuring out the sounds.

Example dialogue:

> **Teacher:** Let's see how many sounds are in the word *cat*.
> **Students:** C…a…t. Three sounds.
> **Teacher:** Three sounds, so I draw three boxes, like this:

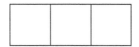

Teacher: Now let's say the word cat slowly and figure out what is the beginning sound in our word.

Students: C…a….t (c/k sound).

Teacher: C — I'm going to slide this block into the first square to show that the first sound is /k/.

(A side note: you don't have to worry about whether it is a *c* or a *k* at this point. We are concerned only about sounds, not letters.)

Repeat the steps to say each sound and slide each block into place.

Teacher: Now let's say our word slowly and point to the blocks in the boxes.

All together: C…a…t.

Teacher: Let's say the word with all the sounds blended together as I run my finger underneath the word more quickly.

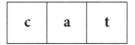

Using Elkonin boxes is a great small-group or individual activity to emphasize concepts that some students may be having difficulty with, such as:

- directionality (left to right within a word);
- beginning sounds;
- vowels;
- looking for sounds across the word;
- saying the word with all the sounds in order.

Some low-prep/high-impact practices that can support your students' learning:

- Make up your own class movements for blending and segmenting sounds in words. You can make it like a special class code that you decide upon together. For example, some classrooms use mimicking stretching a rubber band to provide concrete movements that are done when students are segmenting sounds in words (stretching them out to notice individual sounds). Blending can be shown by saying individual sounds in words and then scooping them up with a finger sweep to mimic putting the sounds together.
- Have the students use handheld mirrors to watch their mouths when they say stop sounds and continuous sounds.
- In your morning meeting, use names to clap syllables, isolate beginning and ending sounds of phonemes, and blend and segment sounds.
- During interactive writing, have students help you when segmenting sounds in words.
- "Guess My Special Word": segment a word and have students blend it together and say it out loud.
- As students are eating a recess snack, walk around and segment snack food words for students to blend together (e.g., pizza, cookies, milk, carrots, raisins, etc.).

Alphabetic Principle

Students often learn the alphabet song even before they begin to attend kindergarten. This mnemonic is also useful to begin to understand that there are letters which are associated with language. However, students may not understand how letters, sounds, and words work in the English language. As noted earlier, it is an abstract concept to connect sounds and letters, and students need to be explicitly and systematically taught how the relationship works between these aspects of language.

Alphabetic Principle can also be referred to as Alphabetic Insight.

The Alphabetic Principle is the idea that the sounds of spoken language are represented by written or printed letters. A student who understands the principle knows that:

- Every spoken word is made up of tiny sounds.
- Every written word is made up of letters.
- Every sound in the words we speak can be represented by a letter or letters.

When students are able to put all these concepts together, an "aha" moment is often evident, and reading and writing become more attainable and concrete. The important concepts to note when making the connections for students explicit is to introduce and reinforce sounds and letters in a sensible order which allows students to begin making words quickly and confidently.

For example, you would want to start with letters that appear often in text, like *m, p, s,* and *t,* and leave the less common letters, such as *q, v, x,* and *z* for later in the learning process. You will also want to introduce at least one vowel letter early on, so students can start building words in their writing.

Many students I have taught, especially at the kindergarten and grade 1 level, did not have the understanding that spoken words and words in print corresponded in the same system (i.e., alphabetic insight). This was very confusing because they thought they needed to learn a whole new way to understand reading and writing. Once those connections were explicitly taught and students had the "aha" moment of connection, the way they approached letters and words changed the organization of their thinking. I remember the look of amazement on one student's face when he looked up at me and said, "This letter is the same one on our alphabet chart and it is the same one that my name begins with." Aha!

We can help students reach the "aha" moment in many different ways:

- Interactive reading and writing are the most natural and engaging way we can explicitly teach alphabetic principle. This requires a lot of modeling and thinking out loud about what is going on in our heads as we solve puzzles and connect sounds to letters. For example, when writing a letter to our buddy class I was able to talk through some of my thought processes when I was writing words. "We are going to invite our buddy class to our classroom to read with us tomorrow. How should we start our sentence?" One student answers, "Do you want to…" "Good idea. Let's write the word do, what sound do you hear first?" "D." "Great I will write a capital D since it is the start of the sentence. What sound do you hear next in the word 'do'? That is a tricky one, let's all say the word and notice the shape of our mouths."
- Take a few minutes a day to reinforce learning that is happening in explicit lessons. Consistency is more important than quantity of time spent on reinforcing. Lining up for recess or handwashing is a great time to fit in a quick review

of learning. I would often say a word in sound segments and have my students blend it together. Once my students were familiar with the routine, I would invite them to say a segmented word and the rest of us would blend it together.

- Start with the simple and build complexity. When we start simple, all students have an on-ramp to learning — it is accessible to everyone. Many students will respond to hearing and saying sounds in words, then adding in letters that make up the sounds in words, and then writing the letters to make up words. Begin to note who needs extra instruction and practice and work with individuals or small groups to reteach concepts and give more guided practice time.

Possible Individual or Small-Group Instruction

If students have very little letter knowledge, begin by introducing the letters in their name. If they have a long name, shorten so you are only working with about five or six letters. Keep coming back to those letters (the letter is *t*, the sound is /t/) and allow for lots of repetition.

Put magnetic letters on a white magnetic board and have students sort the letters based on physical characteristics. The letter sort should be fast and engaging. It works best if the students are standing and they need to use both hands to move the letters around, in order to add some wide arm movements to the activity.

Ways you can have your student sort letters (use different ones each day as students begin to recognize letter names and sounds):

Letter sorts are helpful for students who are struggling with letter reversals.

- letters that make circles;
- letters that have tall backs;
- letters that have tails;
- letters that have curves, straight lines, etc.

After the letter sort, have students point to each letter and say, "The letter name is __; the sound is ___."

Slowly add in new letters as students solidify knowledge, but keep a few known letters at a time, so the students aren't learning all new letters each time.

Phonics Knowledge

Phonics instruction has become a hot topic lately in education and there is a great deal of research and many recommendations to consider as a classroom teacher. I'm going to keep this section short and sweet because I know this subject is much more complex than I have space to explore, given the topic of this book.

For more ideas check out Willms & Alberti's book *This Is How We Teach Reading... And It's Working!*

Phonics is at heart about the relationship between letters and sounds. It does not refer to a specific program; instead, it is instruction that teaches students to work with reading and writing letters while considering their sounds and spelling patterns. Phonics and phonemic awareness are reciprocal skills, and they need to be explicitly woven together to develop significant relationship connections in our working and long-term memory. However, each skill requires its own instruction as well.

There are two types of phonics instruction, synthetic and analytic. A synthetic phonics approach teaches students to convert letters to sounds and then blend the sounds to make a word. This approach emphasizes teaching alphabet knowledge. An analytic phonics approach teaches students to blend the onset (beginning sound) of a word with the rime (rest of the word) into a word using word families. This approach emphasizes teaching word families and is more appropriate for grade 1 or 2 students.

There are many researched and practiced scope and sequences in phonics instruction, describing what you will teach and the order in which you will teach it.

Some clear guidelines you can use to approach a scope and sequence:

- Begin with very simple sound/letter relationships and then move to more complex ones over time so students' learning is building on previous knowledge.
- Begin with predictable sound/letter relationships (letters that have easy sounds to determine based on letter names, such as *t, m, s, f, l*).
- Introduce at least one vowel letter early so students can begin successfully writing words quickly.
- Start with one-syllable words and move slowly to multisyllabic words (you can expose your students to multisyllabic words before they are ready to read or write them, without the expectation that they will be assessed on those words).
- Read longer words in chunks.
- Cycle back to skills to reteach, reinforce, and ensure students have lots of exposure and practice with previously taught skills.

As you teach your phonics scope and sequence, not all students will be learning at the same time. Some students will be far ahead of the rest and spelling out complex sentences while other students will be working on labeling pictures with the beginning letter of a word. That is okay, and the nature of our classrooms. It is important to formatively assess often to see who needs more explicit instruction and guided practice in small groups or individually.

Writing is the best predictor of students' phonics knowledge and the most natural way to gain information about your students' skills. Two quick and easy ways to gather information in a whole-class setting about each student's phonics knowledge are:

1. Simple spelling dictation. Prepare a sentence or two (depending on where your students are in their learning progression) and dictate it to your students. When you are analyzing the students' writing, look for patterns to determine what phonics skills they can apply independently and what skills are missing or incorrect.
2. Interactive writing. Have students join you in interactive writing by writing some words (that you have predetermined) on their own on their individual whiteboards. Students can hold up their whiteboards and you can see at a glance who needs intervention in specific areas.

From these two simple, natural formative assessments, you can pull together small-group intervention instruction that is skill-based and reteach concepts in different ways. For example, if you have a group of students who are struggling with determining the vowel sound in a word, you can bring a bunch of CVC (consonant-vowel-consonant) picture cards to a table and specifically work with the vowel sounds in the middle of the words. A good tip for all students is that every word has a vowel, so they only have five to choose from as they are puzzle-solving.

Classroom Activities to Support Phonics Knowledge

Giant Flash Cards

An interactive way to engage students in applying their phonics knowledge is through the use of giant flash cards. Bring your whole class to a gathering area, like a carpet, and invite some students to come to the front of the class and take a flash card. The flash cards will have single letters and digraphs, depending on the phonics lessons you have taught. The rest of the class will act as "directors". You can say a word and the students will sort themselves out to make the word. The directors have the opportunity to offer input. You can start this process using simple CVC words using only the letters in the word and then progress to more complex words that include digraphs and blends. You can introduce more complexity by adding in extra letters (especially vowels) to students to problem-solve together (Willms & Alberti, 2022).

For example, if you want students to spell the word *play* you can give them both digraphs /ay/ and /ai/ and have them use their knowledge of how words work to problem-solve which one would come at the end of the word.

What Is Different?

Put two words on the board and ask students, "What do you see that is different in these words?"

    ran   /   rain

"What do you hear that is different?"

    cat   /   chat

A close analysis of two words can stimulate thinking for our youngest students, without overwhelming them with a list of words to analyze.

Word Ladders

A simple way for students to practice manipulating letters in words to make new words is though word ladders. Word ladders can focus students to notice and attend across the word to blend each sound. You can do this as a whole-class lesson and easily move it into a small-group intervention for students who need more explicit practice. This is an easy activity that can be practiced in literacy stations as well.

(see template, pg 109)

Have students begin at the top of their word ladder with a word such as *cat*. Ask them to change the *t* to an *n* and tell you the new word they have made (*can*).

Then have them change the *c* to a *b* (*ban*). Keep going as long as students are engaged in the activity.

cat
can
ban
bun
bin
tin
ten
tent

Your students can take over the practice once they learn the format of the activity and make their own words so they can begin to see how to manipulate letters to make new words. You can prompt this by simply saying, "What letter will you change?" They can maintain a sense of control as they become in charge of making new words.

A more sophisticated version of word ladders involves making more complex words through the use of clues. You can introduce this format to your students by preparing a set of clues that will allow students to manipulate letters to make new words. For example:

Start with the month we are in: *May*
Change one letter to make another word for rug: *mat*
Add one letter for a subject that deals with numbers: *math*

Once students become familiar with this activity format, they can come up with their own word ladders and clues and play with peers.

Using Students' Names

Once again, you can engage your youngest learners in noticing different aspects of letters and sounds by studying their own and each other's names. Have all students' names on cards for students' reference and use them to introduce beginning sounds, even if there are non-standard sound-spelling patterns. As your students develop more phonics knowledge, introduce different questions and prompts as ways to engage with names, such as:

- What small words can be made from the letters in each student's name?
- How many syllables are there in each name?
- How can we sort students' names into groups? Beginning sounds? Ending sounds? Short/long vowels? Vowel teams?

Word Wall: I Spy

Whether you create a class word wall or individual word walls, students can engage with the words on them by noticing different aspects of each word. You

Students are very attached to their own names. It is highly motivating to use them when developing phonics knowledge.

(see template, pg 111)

It is beneficial to use word walls and sound walls for different purposes in the classroom.

can give them clues that can include one correct answer or multiple answers and have students study the words to find which word or words match the clues.

Some possible clues:

- The word starts with the letter *t*.
- The word has three letters.
- The word has two syllables.
- The word has a long /e/ sound.
- The word means the opposite of "last".

Word Wall	
Aa all am and are	**Bb** be because big but
Cc can can't come children	**Dd** day did do down
Ee eat	**Ff** favorite for friend from
Gg get girl give good	**Hh** had have he here
Ii in is it	**Jj** jump
Kk kick	**Ll** like little look

Mm	Nn
made	new
make	nice
me	night
my	not

Oo	Pp
of	people
off	play
old	pretty
out	

Qq	Rr
quit	rain
	ride

Ss	Tt
said	talk
saw	teacher
school	that
she	thing

Uu	Vv
up	very
us	

Ww	Xx, Yy, Zz
want	you
was	your
what	zoo
why	

This activity can be easily differentiated to include some basic high-frequency words and more complex words that may fit into the clue categories. Students can help by coming up with their own clues and share with the whole class or a partner during literacy stations.

Decoding Skills

An important aspect of phonics is the application of knowledge through decoding words in explicit lessons and in reading decodable texts. Decoding is the application of knowledge built through phonics lessons to use letter-sound relationships to pronounce words when reading. When students are decoding, they are using all their foundational skills to recognize new words, generally by blending sounds.

Emphasizing decoding when we are connecting to word recognition allows students to practice what they have learned in connected text. The purpose of teaching word recognition to students is so they can use their skills in text, not in isolation. When students hear a word pronounced and see the visual representation of the word — the spelling — those areas of the brain are linked and provide a stronger connection in the brain.

It is important to explicitly and systematically teach phonetic rules and understanding because most students cannot figure them out on their own. The systematic aspect of instruction is important as we teach new information because students learn best when specific phonics skills are taught in relation to the overall spelling system that students are learning. The key components are naturally mapped out in order from simple to more complex. Instruction follows routines that students become comfortable with and provides a structure they come to know and expect. Knowledge of phonics helps teachers make logical decisions about how to introduce new information.

Classroom Activities That Strengthen Decoding Skills

Lesson Format

A quick lesson format that can emphasize the phonics lessons you have recently taught can look similar to the following steps:

1. Remind students what phonics concept you are focusing on in this lesson.
2. Introduce a decodable text that is connected to the phonics focus.
3. Practice the first page together through an "echo" read.
4. Allow students to continue reading the rest of the book in a whisper, silently, or into a whisper phone (if that is helpful for the student).
5. Conference with students to ensure they are applying phonics knowledge when word-solving.
6. Offer praise points at the end of the lesson by saying something like, "I noticed Jake stopped for a moment and thought about what we learned today."
7. Continue with individual reading time by inviting students to choose what they would like to focus on: "Would you like to continue to read a different decodable book that we have previously practiced? Or keep practicing this one? Or read one of your books in your book bag that we worked on choosing together?"

This lesson format is quick and focused and allows students to have plenty of time practicing reading.

This lesson format is quick and focused and allows students to have plenty of time practicing reading, rather than having a lot of random phonics activities that may be confusing or disjointed for your students. By using decodable texts, you are emphasizing the phonics concepts through reading connected texts. Essentially, decodable texts are used as an application of phonics knowledge — they are a tool. I've heard decodable books referred to as training wheels for beginning readers. Rich, interesting literature also needs to be an active part of literacy instruction in the classroom in order for many of the language comprehension concepts and strategies to be taught and practiced by your students.

Encoding and Decoding

It is important to teach encoding (writing) at the same time you teach decoding (reading) because when you are teaching a specific decoding lesson, you can easily add a writing component. The writing activity should prompt students to write the same elements of text that students have just learned, so they will make connections between reading and writing and the learning will be strengthened.

Reciprocity between reading and writing is a very important aspect of written language. The systems in your brain that promote writing a word and reading a word are not individual parts of the brain that don't talk to each other. When you are thinking about writing a word, you are activating similar pathways connecting the meaning of the word, the pronunciation of the word, and the spelling of the word.

Choosing Decodable Texts

Using a decodable text is not a substitute for good stories or for deep comprehension. We need to use other books for that learning. Decodable texts are most useful at the first-grade level when students are learning important phonics skills. Students need to practice reading connected text that is focused on the phonics skills in order to automatize those skills.

When you are choosing which decodable texts to use with your students, you may want to consider the following questions:

- Are the stories worth thinking about?
- Do the phonics used in the books follow a clear scope and sequence that makes sense to you?
- Are the books engaging enough to hold students' attention?
- Do the books make sense? Are students able to understand the story?
- Are the books instructive so students will learn from them?
- Are there a variety of books that emphasize similar phonics concepts?

When you make the reciprocity between decoding and encoding explicit and evident to students, you can strengthen those connections in the brain so students can see that they can use phonics knowledge to both read and write. It is important for students to know that reading, writing, and speaking are all using the same alphabetic principle.

Spelling Word Analysis

Spelling word analysis can give teachers a view into a student's mind. Seeing what phonetic skills students can reproduce easily or partially can assist teachers in having a clear path forward to support each student with what they need. The spelling words will be determined by what phonetic skills have been taught. For example, if the word is *chat* and the student writes *cat* they will need some instruction in the *ch* digraph.

Teachers can specifically point out when students are using foundational skills in decoding by making a reinforcing statement such as:

- "I can see you are using what we learned at the beginning of the year about syllables as you clap the word you are spelling."
- "It's tricky to figure out which vowel goes in the middle; it looks like you were thinking about the shape of your mouth when you were saying the word you were writing."

- "You wrote most of those words automatically; that means you have them in your memory. The ones you don't have in your memory yet are the ones you are having some problems with."

Decoding lessons should be short and engaging; however, the application of those decoding concepts should last across the whole day.

Decoding throughout the Day

Here are some examples of cross-curricular practice in decoding:

- In a science lesson about weather, you can say, "Let's build some words about weather using what we already know about letter sounds and spellings."
- While reading a book about seasons, you can ask students, "What information did the author want us to pay attention to? Students answer, "The highlighted words." You can respond, "Let's take a look at those words now and see if we can read and write them."
- When students arrive in the morning, have them read the daily question and then ask some of them to write their answers on the board. *Would you rather go skiing or swimming? Would you rather have a dog or a cat as a pet? What word did you learn over the weekend?*

Applying phonics knowledge is not just something we should do during phonics lessons. Rather, it can impact everything we do throughout the day.

Recognition of Words at Sight

Essentially most words will become sight words. As students store more and more words in their long-term memory, ready for automatic retrieval, they become sight words. I will use the term high-frequency words to describe the words found often in text. High-frequency word instruction is important because many of the words students encounter as they read beginning texts will need to be explicitly taught. Our students will need to know enough words on a page to make meaning and connect to previous knowledge. When you see a word, your brain activates what you know about that word when it is spoken (pronunciation, meaning); therefore, word recognition isn't just a visual process. According to Burkins and Yates (2021), 109 high-frequency words make up 50 percent of the words found in children's texts. As teachers, we are setting our students up for success when we explicitly teach high-frequency words and refer to them often in our instruction.

Orthographic Mapping

One way we can explicitly teach high-frequency words that have irregular sound-spelling patterns is with a process called orthographic mapping (Ehri, 2014). Orthographic mapping is essentially connecting sounds in spoken words with the sound spellings and putting those connections into long-term memory. Because humans typically learn to speak before they learn to read, we often have the pronunciation of words already in our long-term memory, so we need to align the spelling to the pronunciation.

An example script of an orthographic mapping lesson:

Decoding practice does not end when the literacy block is over.

- I have a very important word to teach you today. It is the word "does". A sentence with the word "does" in it can sound like this: "Does your brother wash the dishes at home?" Now, turn to your elbow partner and tell them a sentence that has the word "does" in it.
- How many sounds are in the word "does"? Three sounds: I will make three boxes on the board.
- Now let's think about the sounds in the word "does". What is the first sound you hear? /d/. I will write the letter *d* in the first sound box. What is the second sound you hear in the word "does"? /uh/. What letter do you think it is? This is such a surprise! In the word "does", we have the letter *o* in the second sound box. What is the third sound in the word "does"? /z/. What letter do you think it is? Wow, we have another surprise! We need to put the letters *es* in our third sound box. Isn't that wonderful, we have two surprises in this word. We will need to put two hearts, one in the second box and one in the third box, to remind us that those are surprises we need to learn by heart.
- Write the word "does" on your individual white boards. Does your word look like mine?

To reinforce the process of orthographic mapping of the word "does", you can:

- have the word on a word card that students touch and say as they exit the room at the end of the day;
- make sure the word is part of your daily morning message and interactive writing for the next few days or weeks;
- add it to your word wall.

There are of course far too many words that students encounter daily to use the process of orthographic mapping on every word. You will need to prioritize which words are important enough to use valuable classroom instruction time to teach explicitly. Consider the high-frequency word lists (such as the one by Burkins and Yates mentioned earlier) and make some decisions.

If words are:

- regular spelling that students can use their phonics knowledge to decode — do not teach.
- irregular spelling but they are not used much in daily texts — do not necessarily teach unless they are part of a topic you are studying.
- irregular spelling and found often in texts — teach through orthographic mapping.

Example dialogue during an interactive writing lesson when I am sharing the pen with a student as they write the word "does":

Marco starts to sound out the word "does".
Sasha: No, remember, that is the heart part. We have to go into our memory to get that part.
Dale: You have to ask yourself, does that look right? Does it match with my memory?
Marco spells the word "does".

Teacher: I see you are getting into your memory. Let's double-check against the word wall. Can you find the word "does"? Are you right?

Marco, Sasha, and Dale: shouts of enthusiasm!

Word recognition involves much more than being able to correctly say words when reading. As you can see from this chapter, there are many different aspects to word recognition for our students to learn in order to gain automaticity. There is a sense of playing with sounds and words that may help students discover how language works. Phonological awareness development can be made playful and interesting by learning aspects of language through songs, poems, and rhymes. Alphabetic insight requires some explicit teaching to connect sounds, letters, and words. Phonics, decoding, and high-frequency words are examined outside of connected text often, and then practiced within connected text.

In the next chapter we will dive into language comprehension and how the different aspects of language affect our overall ability to read and make sense of what we are reading. We will explore all the thinking that goes on in the brain of a reader through the background knowledge in areas of content and culture, as well as reading specific features. We will take a close look at how language works to reveal connections, emotions, diverse perspectives through verbal reasoning, language structure, and theory of mind.

4

Language Comprehension

> When children pay attention to the evolving meaning as they read and create new ways to think about and share the information later, there is a significant improvement in their ability to remember books and transfer the information they've synthesized to new learning situation.
> — Ellin Oliver Keene and Susan Zimmerman, *Mosaic of Thought*, (p. 234–235)

Language comprehension is the ability of students to understand the language around them, including conversation and read-alouds. Language conversation is practice within an oral language environment, so the ability for students to rely on their oral language knowledge is crucial to their language development. Language comprehension starts at birth and continues to develop for years as we encounter more complex language and concepts. Since language comprehension works in the oral language space, early language development is foundational for later reading success. Students gain language comprehension skills through many interactions they have with conversations, books read to them, and cultural events they participate in. All our students come to us with funds of knowledge that are unique to them.

Students can generally understand more (and more complex) language than they can express through oral language. They need lots of exposure to language of various levels of complexity and lots of practicing with appropriate scaffolds in place. Getting students to talk and respond in a dialogue format builds their listening and representing skills through oral language. Conversation that is intentional and meaningful is needed in the early years.

An important method of continuing the learning process after reading a text is to set up opportunities — formal or informal — for playful interactions with the content, concepts, characters, or topics brought up in the text. "When young children apply the new knowledge they're learning into their play, they extend their learning in ways that are motivating and meaningful" (Duke, 2023).

Why is talk so important? First and foremost, it provides a window into who our students are and what they think. Also, talking not only promotes

Language comprehension starts at birth and continues to develop for years as we encounter more complex language and concepts.

relationships and community building within a classroom but also provides significant academic payoffs in learning. Talking supports robust learning by boosting memory and providing richer connections to concepts through vocabulary development. Conversations allow students to have a voice and encourages them to reason with evidence. In addition, intentional talk can enrich the development of critical social skills in and out of the classroom. What follows are strategies and activities to support intentional talk and language comprehension in the early years' classroom.

Cultural and Other Content Knowledge

One of the first steps people take when they approach text is to activate their background knowledge. However, what happens if they don't have the background knowledge to activate? A lack of content knowledge obviously impacts comprehension. All students have different background knowledge as it is built through experience, culture, language, environment, and many other factors.

In the early years we need to start building content knowledge for all our students to set them up for success when they encounter a variety of texts later on in their reading journey. The good news is that students don't need to be experts on a topic in order to comprehend text. They just need enough basic knowledge to make some connections, think about some questions they have, and gather a few details that will help with entry into the new concepts.

Vocabulary is also a component of background knowledge. As teachers think about what vocabulary words are important to teach, we can think about which vocabulary words are important to understand the concept we are exploring with students. Also, we can think about teaching vocabulary words that are connected to each other, to further develop concept knowledge.

Building content knowledge takes time, so know it is okay to go slowly and go deeper into concepts. Students will develop their knowledge at different rates and to different depths according to their motivation and engagement.

Students want to learn new information and build their knowledge. Building knowledge is highly engaging. Students can listen to teachers talk and process information, but so much more learning can happen when students take that new knowledge and talk to other students or adults about it. This is where we can set up intentional conversation time.

We need to engage with students around reading to build content and cultural knowledge very early on in their reading journey, so they get the idea that reading is about building knowledge.

Cultural Knowledge

Reading is impacted by text, task, and sociocultural context.

Teachers have the power and influence to ensure cultural diversity is honored and practiced in our classrooms. Through the lens of critical literacy, we can teach students to read between the lines when reading texts and ask important questions, whether they are reading culturally based texts or other texts.

Students can question the content of a story and nuances or inferences that may be evident just below the surface. They can be prompted by the following questions:

- Whose story is this?
- Who benefits from this story?
- Who is not being heard?

These questions support students' thinking beyond the text to consider deep meaning and impact of text on cultural knowledge. Teachers can read books beforehand to anticipate meaning and questions or concepts that may come up in different cultures. It is important to intentionally leave time and space for students to talk and discuss what they are noticing about the texts, as well as responding to the questions written above. To ensure you are setting your students up for learning about diverse cultures, you can have a variety of texts in your classroom or library, so students can develop some background knowledge about cultural context.

It is important to expand students' vocabulary so they broaden their understanding of cultural diversity. It takes some time and commitment to not only expose students to culturally diverse books but also to discuss them within a respectful classroom community. Building background knowledge begins with becoming aware of one's own culture alongside different cultures. This kind of cultural knowledge goes beyond learning about elements of culture such as food, dress, music, and holidays. Even with our youngest learners, we can introduce concepts outlined in the BC Language Arts curriculum, such as these:

- Stories and texts help us learn about ourselves and our families.
- Through listening and speaking, we connect with others and share our world.
- Curiosity and wonder lead us to new discoveries about ourselves and the world around us.

For example, I recently worked with a grade 1 class and used the book *A Day with Yayah*, written by Nicola Campbell, as a read-aloud to prompt conversation about generational learning and the importance of language. The story is about a First Nations family that goes on an outing to gather edible plants and mushrooms. Through the story the grandmother teaches the children how to say specific words in the Nłeʔkepmxcín language.

Throughout the reading of the story, students asked if we could find similar plants and mushrooms in the area they lived in. We decided to do some investigation through conversations with our families at home, and then gather the next day and discuss what we found out. After we made an action plan, some other questions started to surface.

> **Teacher:** We can learn a lot about ourselves and our families as we read books together. What connections are you making to your family?
>
> **Taina:** I go on hikes with my family in the summer and we look for huckleberries. My dad goes first, just in case there are bears. Bears like to eat huckleberries too.
>
> **Quan:** At home we speak Korean and I ask my grandma how to say things, just like the children did in the story. But there are lots of books written in Korean that we have at our house and we sing songs in my language too.
>
> **Kai:** You are so lucky to speak two languages, we only speak one at home. But my neighbours are from Hong Kong and they sometimes give me yummy treats to eat that don't taste like anything I've had before.

Taina: Why don't the children in the book just read books to learn their language?

Teacher: I don't think the Nłe?kepmxcín language is written down in books like many other languages. The grandmother passes down her knowledge of the language through speaking it to the children.

Taina: How can it not be written down? You mean, they can't find books in their language?

Kai: It is like what you told us about many Indigenous languages not being spoken when children went to residential schools, like in the book where the brothers and sisters went away and they snuck away to meet each other.

Teacher: Are you thinking about the book *When We Were Alone*, by David Robertson [shows the cover]?

Kai: Yes, they couldn't speak their language, they had to say their words in secret.

Taina: They would get in trouble if they spoke their language. That's probably why it is not written down more and why the grandmother is teaching the children.

Quan: The children must be sad they don't know more of the language. I know I would be. I love speaking Korean with my family.

Talking and listening are how most students learn. Conversations similar to the one outlined above allow students to have the time and space to impact their thinking about concepts that are familiar or unfamiliar. Young students are great questioners, more so than many older students, and they seem generally comfortable asking other people questions and listening to each other's perspectives.

Background knowledge, in the early years, is developed through oral language and language comprehension. Vocabulary is developed at a much earlier stage than reading. Students are set up to anticipate meaning when they are reading and writing. Students who can understand vocabulary in context, infer, and learn from what they read are set up to continue to learn as they encounter more complex texts. "Knowledgeable readers are more effective readers, and more effective readers can more easily build knowledge for reading and writing" (Duke, 2023, blog).

Content Knowledge

Text can be used as a catalyst for curiosity about a subject, place, event, or person. The options are endless. Once a child reads about a topic, they can wonder about different aspects of the topic and continue to search for new information based on their wonderings. Research can take the form of internet searches, but it can also be further reading (informational or narrative) about a subject to gain a better understanding and fuel the students' sense of curiosity.

If we want to engage and motivate our students, we need to provide them with opportunities to learn about what they are interested in learning about. To truly "hook" our students, we can give them an extended period of time to learn more about a topic or concept by allowing them to respond to a question they have, solve a real problem, or consider a real need. Authenticity is highly motivating. Authenticity also allows for differentiation in interests, abilities, perspectives, and beliefs. As teachers, we need to expand our students' content knowledge, but we don't need to expand it in the same way, with the same information, for each student. Our students are pretty good at guiding us and allowing us to be co-researchers. In the student's mind, the teacher is working with them to further expand their knowledge to continue the learning about their project. Often there are specific reading and writing requirements students need to develop along their journey and the teacher acts as a resource to develop those specific literacy skills at the time they are needed.

One day in my grade 3 class, a student named Gemma came into the classroom with a grim look on her face. When I asked her what was bothering her, she said that there was a problem with one of the geese that lived close to her house on a lake. After she told me the gist of the problem, I suggested that she might want to bring it up during our morning meeting to see if anyone had any ideas.

Gemma spoke up during the morning meeting.

> **Gemma:** Last night my dad and I saw a goose with an arrow sticking through its wing. I feel worried about the goose, but I don't know what to do about it.

> Students asked a variety of questions: Did you see blood? Can the goose walk? Swim? How could someone shoot an arrow at a goose — isn't that illegal? Did the goose have babies with it?

> Gemma asked if she could find out some answers to everyone's questions and talk about the situation again the following day.

> The next morning Gemma came in brimming with new information.

> **Gemma:** I saw the goose again and found out that it can swim and walk okay, but my dad and I don't think it can fly. It did not have babies with it, but there are lots of gaggles of goslings around the lake right now. I asked my dad if it was illegal and he thought it was but we weren't sure what authorities to phone. Does anyone have any suggestions?

A small group of students showed interest in doing some research about the wounded goose and a project was born. I worked with the small group to facilitate some questions they wanted answers to through the research.

The questions they came up with were:

- Can geese survive without being able to fly?
- What will happen when the geese migrate in the fall? (We had learned about animal life cycles previously in the year, so the students were building on prior knowledge.)
- How do we make sure no one else shoots arrows at geese in the future?

The first two questions required some research. We consulted diagrams of geese to look closely at the construction of their wings. I found some informational books about geese in the library to potentially answer the questions. The certified education assistant in the classroom searched for some informational videos on geese. We invited a conservation officer into the classroom for an informational session.

The answers we found out from our research:

- Geese will have a hard time surviving without the ability to fly, especially when it gets closer to migration time.

Often our students' experiences prompt the learning that happens in our classrooms.

- There is the possibility that the goose could work out the arrow on its own by biting it and moving it around.
- It is very difficult and dangerous to try to catch a goose, especially a wounded one.
- In terms of the last question, the conservation officer explained that it is not okay to shoot arrows at geese and the public needs to hear that message.

The last course of action we took was to write a letter to be printed in the school newsletter. I facilitated a shared writing exercise which all students participated in, but the small group acted as the knowledgeable group that informed the rest about their learning. We decided that it was not enough to just write, "Don't shoot arrows at birds": we needed to provide the reasons why.

Our final letter read like this:

Dear Students and Families,

We need to tell you some upsetting news. There is a wounded goose that lives close to the school. Someone shot it with an arrow and the arrow is stuck in its wing. The goose cannot fly and that means it will probably not survive when it gets close to migration season in the fall.

We ask you not to shoot arrows at any birds because:

- When they are wounded, they become very vulnerable and might get eaten by predators.
- It is probably very painful to have a wounded wing.
- They will miss their gaggles when they start to migrate.
- If the wounded goose has goslings, the goslings might not survive.
- When the person shot the arrow, they might have hit other animals or humans.

Please don't shoot arrows at birds. And tell everyone you know.

Thank you,

Mrs. Kelly's Grade 3 Class

Wonder Hour

I appreciate the use of the word "wonder" because it is invitational.

I visited a classroom recently where the teacher introduced the concept of "wonder hour". Each student was invited to "wonder" about a topic that they wanted to find out more information about during wonder hour. This routine was going to be a year-long process. Many students chose topics that they had some background knowledge of and wanted to learn more about by exploring different questions they had. Some students chose topics that they had learned about from reading books (narrative and informational). The topics ranged from how to build a canoe to the migration patterns of grizzly bears. The teacher acted as a research assistant by helping students search for information in various sources and in a variety of text complexity to meet students where they were in their reading ability. If a student wanted to change their wonder topic, they were welcome to do so. Each student would have a meeting scheduled with the teacher to discuss their project and what they needed assistance with to continue the research. The teacher would document the students' words and keep track of each student's journey.

Story Workshop

A popular method to connect text to play is through story workshop. Story workshop is a structure that supports language and literacy development. Teachers work alongside students as they explore prepared environments or experiences.

Through story workshop students can start to understand that they:

- can be curious about the environment around them;
- are competent communicators;
- have important stories to tell;
- can make connections to other people's stories;
- have big emotions they can explore and share with others.
  (MacKay, 2021)

With a grade 1 class, I introduced the book *And Tango Makes Three*, by Justin Richardson and Peter Parnell. The story is a narrative story about a true event involving penguins in the Central Park Zoo in New York City. Two penguins want to be like the other couples who are sitting on eggs and waiting for them to hatch. An employee notices this and gets an egg that was abandoned by another penguin. The family unit happily raises their "adopted" penguin.

When we finished reading the story and had in-depth conversations about the penguins and the concepts of family that were raised by the students, I asked the students, "How can we continue this learning?"

Janelle: We can read more about penguins in different books.

Thomas: Can we make penguin characters and use them in our story workshop bins?

Mark: Yeah, we can build zoo pools and areas for penguins to build nests!

Teacher: What kind of materials shall we gather? Janelle, you mentioned some books on penguins. Do you want to go see Mr. Timms in the library and see if he can help you out?

Janelle: Sure! [Happily walks out of the classroom.]

Mark: I think we'll need rocks for the nests and some containers to put water in.

Saniya: We definitely need some penguin characters. Could we gather some sticks and give them the penguin names?

The students engaged with the materials in different ways. Some students recreated the story of *And Tango Makes Three* within a zoo setting developed with various materials. Some students chose to develop their own stories about penguins living in the wild. An interesting conversation came up when one student was looking at the National Geographic Kids book titled *Penguins!* written by Anne Schreiber. Nadia read that penguins live between the equator and the south pole, then she asked some students at her table, "But why did the story take place in New York City if penguins don't live there?" I asked her to bring up her question during our Share Out time that afternoon. After Nadia asked her question to the whole class and explained her thinking, we had a robust conversation about zoos and taking animals away from their natural habitat.

Interactive Read-Alouds in Science and Social Studies:

Interactive read-alouds are an engaging way to invite students into learning about new concepts in science and social studies. Reading aloud expands vocabulary knowledge while placing new words in context so students have a greater understanding of those words. A few key questions throughout a book can give students the opportunity to consider their thinking around new knowledge and inspire them to want to learn more. Not only does a read-aloud teach new content, but it also reinforces a proficient reader's strategy use when a teacher models their thinking throughout the book.

I was teaching a grade 1 class of enthusiastic environmentalists when the topic of water pollution came up. I jumped at the chance to explore the concept further as the topic of the relationship between a community and its environment is one the learning standards in the BC curriculum for grade 1 social studies. My students were already motivated to learn more and fully engaged in the topic, so the timing was perfect. I decided to begin my teaching through a read-aloud of the story *Ducks Overboard: A True Story of Plastic in Our Oceans,* by Markus Motum. The story is brilliantly written as both a narrative and informational book. It is a true account of a container ship that lost a container full of plastic toys that fell overboard during the long journey from China to the United States in 1992. The fictional element is that the story is told from the point of view of one of the plastic ducks and the adventure it went on and the things it saw in the ocean before ending up in the Great Pacific Garbage Patch and eventually on a beach filled with garbage. Throughout the book there are informational sentences written in a different font to distinguish them from the narrative storyline.

When I was reading the book to my students, I pointed out the clever way the author told the story and gave information at the same time. I picked out three different points where I planned to stop and discuss new vocabulary that would further develop content knowledge for my students. We discussed currents in oceans, single-use plastic, and recycling. My students had many questions about the use of plastics and how garbage could impact the lake the community was close to.

To continue our learning, I decided on another book to read aloud a few days later. The book I chose was called *We Are Water Protectors*, by Carole Lindstrom. The story describes how women in the Ojibwe culture are the protectors of water. It highlights the importance of water for life and why it needs to be protected so it is as clean as it was for the ancestors. The people describe a black snake that threatens to destroy the land. My grade 1 students were mesmerized when we figured out together that the black snake was an analogy for pollution. We also discussed in depth what it means to be stewards of the earth. They connected the story to their new knowledge from *Ducks Overboard* and what we had learned about Indigenous culture and the importance of land, water, and community.

Reading-Specific Background Knowledge (Genre, Text Features, Etc.)

Reading involves much more than decoding text. Books are set up in particular ways to provide focus on different ways to read and gain knowledge. Different genres are set up differently and that is why we need to expose students to many genres early in their reading journey; otherwise they may think all reading involves narrative text that tells a story. Even within narrative texts, there are different ways authors choose to set up text, such as *Ducks Overboard* described in the previous section. Having reading-specific background knowledge can set students up for a successful reading experience as they encounter different ways to present information, describe events, and engage the reader.

Text features are an important feature of many informational books. If students are not explicitly taught how to read text features, they may miss out on important information highlighted within books. When I think about my early classroom teaching, I realize I had far more narrative books in my classroom library than informational books. And when I consider my reading as an adult, I tend to read a lot more informational text than narrative on a daily basis. I read informational text to learn about current events, how to make a cake, how loons can dive so deep, what the significance of algae blooms are in lakes, and, of course, what is current reading research. Introducing students early on to such texts can hone a skill that will impact their life-long learning.

Informational Text Features

There are many simple informational texts that are helpful when teaching students the purpose of text features and how to use them to obtain new knowledge. I highlight different text features in read-alouds, explaining what I learn when reading a caption, a photo, a diagram, and subtitles within text. You can ask your students specific questions about their learning or wondering as you read. For example, if you are reading an informational book, you can ask your students, "Why do you think the author chose this photo to include in this section of the book?" It is important for students to understand that text features in books are there to aid comprehension.

Informational text features are there to help the reader comprehend the text.

A table of contents is an important feature to engage students in the information they are going to encounter in the specific chapters or parts of a book. My students were amazed when I explained that they can jump to a chapter they are most interested in learning about and share their new knowledge with the rest of the class or group. Informational texts do not necessarily need to be read in order from front to back. This fact empowered my students to take charge of their learning and they felt a sense of pride when they could share their expertise with other students.

For example, in the National Geographic Kids book *Cats vs. Dogs*, by Elizabeth Carney, students in a grade 2 class enjoyed first deciding whether they preferred cats or dogs, and then learning about a specific aspect of the different animals. In a small group I was teaching, I shared the table of contents at the beginning of the book and asked each student what they were most interested in learning about. They each chose a chapter to read and then we gathered back together to have a discussion.

> **Carey:** I totally knew dogs would have a better sense of smell because my dog sniffs everything when my dad and I take him out for walks. Sometimes we can't even get him to move he is so interested in what he is smelling.
>
> **Jordan:** Yeah, I read that chapter too, but I was surprised that cats can hear better than dogs because my dog barks at everyone who walks past the house, even if she can't see them. But the book says that cats hear sounds that humans and dogs never even notice.
>
> **Molly:** I learned what the word "instinct" means in my chapter. It means having some behaviors that animals are born knowing how to do. I wonder if humans have instincts?

Kristy: Yeah, of course we do. My little brother knew how to drink milk from my mother's breast right when he was born — that's what my mom said.

As children understand the importance of constantly thinking about the meaning of the text, as they develop their skills as readers, they will encounter more complex ideas to consider.

Dialogic Reading

A reading process that invites students to be active participants in reading is dialogic reading. Rather than reading to children and having them listen passively, dialogic reading invites students into the space of wonder and curiosity by putting the children into a position of co-storytellers. Children learn more when they are actively involved in the text, and dialogic reading allows them to make meaning through knowledge-building. They can take ownership of their own ideas and connections to the text.

A dialogic classroom can be described as setting up intentional ways for students to dialogue. Dialogue is more formal than simply a conversation. It denotes a way for students to be active listeners and responders by building on each other's ideas and thoughts. It is a lifelong skill that leads to new ways to think about things differently. It really is about democracy and the importance of building understandings together as a community of learners (Johnston, 2012).

Whitehurst (2015) describes the process of creating dialogue through the acronym PEER.

- Prompt the child to say something about the text.
- Evaluate the child's response.
- Expand the child's response by using the child's words and adding information to the child's response.
- Repeat the prompt to make sure the child has learned from the expansion.

An example of the process is:

> **Teacher:** What is happening in this picture?
> **Child:** A dog is jumping into the water.
> **Teacher:** The brown dog is jumping into the water. It looks like a stream in the forest. What is the dog doing?
> **Child:** He is jumping into the stream in the forest.

Whitehurst suggests some different prompts that will allow children to become involved in the storytelling of the text and enhance their oral language development through vocabulary extension and context. The prompts connect to the acronym CROWD.

- Completion prompts are usually used with repetitive or rhyming books. Reading aloud, the adult leaves a blank at the end of the sentence, and the child fills it in using cues from the structure of the language they have heard in the book.
- Recall prompts are questions about a book the child has already read. These prompts assist children in understanding the story plot and describing events.

- Open-ended prompts focus on the pictures in books and work best with rich, detailed illustrations. This kind of prompt gives children opportunities to increase their expressive fluency and add detail.
- Wh- prompts begin with what, where, when, why, and how and often focus on the pictures in books to teach children new vocabulary.
- Distancing prompts relate to pictures or words in the book that connect to experiences outside it. Distancing prompts allow students to use background knowledge or experiences to build a relationship between the child and the text.

When using a dialogic reading process, ensure that the conversation between adult and child is authentic. The process invites children to become co-story-tellers through intention and practice in meaningful ways that encourage and promote oral language development and a sense of curiosity about texts.

Dialogic engagement can improve students'

- ability to see others' perspectives;
- reasoning ability in math and science;
- ability to think critically;
- language comprehension;
- ability to build arguments;
- expressive language;
- creative thinking.

Dialogic engagement within a classroom allows is associated with positive social behaviours and sensitivity to others but also with higher self-esteem and lower anxiety (Johnston et al., 2020).

Short Story Lesson Activity

Using a short story, pick out seven or eight key sentences and put them on sentence strips. Dividing the class into small groups, model the process of putting the sentences in a possible order that may develop a storyline. Give each group the same sentence strips and discuss what may make sense based on their discussions about a potential storyline. Give students a choice of how many sentences they would like to use. They may want to focus on choosing three sentences to put in order, or for more of a challenge they can choose five sentences they want to work with, or they can try to work with all the sentences. If you allow students to have choice in this activity, they all have an entry point into the work and consequently they show more motivation to engage in the process. Team up each group with another group and give the groups time to explain their work and the thinking behind it to each other. Each group's job is to listen carefully to the other and ask questions. Students complete this pre-reading activity with a high level of motivation to read the short story (or listen to the story), to confirm their ideas, or change their theories as they gain new information.

In the short story "Monkey's Paw" by W.W. Jacobs, I used the following sentence strips to pique my students' interest and get them thinking about a possible story plot. (The actual story is about a preserved monkey's paw that can grant three wishes.)

> "And what is there special about it?" inquired Mr. White as he took it from his son, and having examined it, placed in upon the table.

Students will be highly motivated to find out if their theories about the text are correct.

"Why, we're going to be rich, and famous, and happy."

"But for all that, the thing moved in my hand; that I'll swear to."

"Might drop on his head from the sky," said the frivolous Herbert.

"Never mind, though; there's no harm done, but it gave me a shock all the same."

"I wish for two hundred pounds," said the old man distinctly.

"THE PAW!" she cried wildly. "THE MONKEY'S PAW!"

Information Picture Book Lesson Activity

(see template, pg 113)

Model looking at a photo from a non-fiction book. Make a T-chart on the board. What do you see? What does this make you wonder? I used a photo from *Hummingbird Book*, written by Donald and Lillian Stokes, to develop some wonderings with my students while learning about birds in the area where we live.

What do you see?	What does this make you wonder?
I see many different colors of hummingbirds.	I wonder if they all eat from the same feeder?
I see flowers beside the feeders.	I wonder if hummingbirds prefer flower nectar or sugar water?
I see the hummingbird's long beak.	I wonder if hummingbids all have long beaks?

This activity encourages students to focus on the aspects of the photo (concrete thinking) and consider how they can interact with the image to develop wonderings (conceptual thinking). Have students do this activity individually or in small groups. Then read the text connected to the photo or the whole book, and discuss whether any of the students' wonderings were answered by the text. Do they have any new wonderings that developed as they learned further information? Such discussion encourages flexible thinking and engagement through curiosity.

Notebook Responding

All students can engage with the text in a way that works for them.

Ensure all students have a blank notebook (or just pieces of paper stapled together) that they can use as their "read-aloud notebook". When students are invited to the carpet or read-aloud area in the classroom, they will all bring their notebooks and pencils with them. As students are listening to the book the teacher is reading, they are invited to respond in their notebooks in ways that work for them to engage with the content or story. Students may draw settings or characters, make notes in words or sentences, write questions or wonderings, doodle images that relate to their thinking. All students can engage with the text in a way that works for them.

Discuss beforehand how students will use their notebooks to better understand the text (this is another way to set goals and create a sense of accountability).

Afterward, discuss with students how their work during the reading helped them focus or think deeply about the text.

> **Teacher:** Who would like to share how you worked in your notebook when we were reading *Watercress*, by Andrea Wang?
>
> **Wendy:** I decided to write the words that you were saying loudly when you were reading, like "look" and "watercress" and "fresh" and "free". I tried my best to spell them.
>
> **Jagmeet:** I decided to try and imagine what watercress looked like and draw it.
>
> **Moira:** When it got to the sad part when the mom was talking about her brother, I made some teardrops on my paper and wrote the word "sad".
>
> **Derry:** I'm working on drawing faces, so I drew the faces of the characters. I made the girl's face sad, the brother was goofy, and the parents were both happy with memories.

Verbal Reasoning (Inference, Metaphor, Etc.)

Verbal reasoning involves a student's ability to understand and reason using words — essentially thinking with words. In terms of reading, it encompasses deeper understanding than what the text states. It is what is meant by *reading between the lines*.

This is a sophisticated cognitive skill that can be taught and strengthened in many ways in the classroom. Generally, students will need to be able to draw conclusions from limited information or look beyond words to infer meaning. As our youngest students begin to comprehend text, they will start with literal knowledge that is evident in the text, but there are ways we can invite them to consider a new way to read.

A very natural way to invite students to think beyond the text is to encourage their questions. Students are very good question askers, especially in the early years. Often when I read a book to students, I do not even have to prompt their questions. They are naturally curious and ask many questions, such as Why? Why not? How come? That is my opening to go further and deeper into the text to consider those questions.

During a read-aloud of the book *Our Table*, by Peter H. Reynolds, to grade 1 students, I had many questions from students throughout the reading. The story is about a family that is increasingly spending time on electronic devices or in front of the TV, rather than interacting with each other. The main character, Violet, notices the decrease in interaction, specifically eating dinner together, but the rest of the family does not. As the family continues to be absorbed in their devices, the family table gets smaller and smaller until it vanishes. Violet sets out to fix the situation by asking the members of her family for help building a new table. As the family works together, they become more connected and realize how much happier they are. I stopped at the part where the table vanishes and many hands went up to try and understand why it had. I explained to the students that the author does not explicitly say that the table disappeared because the family was disconnected, but why do you think that? What are the clues in the book? The students continued to notice different things throughout the book that gave us clues about the backstory, what was happening behind the scenes that was not necessarily explained in the text. They noticed that as the family got more connected, the pictures started to have color in them until the final picture that was the most colorful of all — when the family was eating dinner at their new table.

Curiosity is a significant component of verbal reasoning. Students need to be curious about something to go beyond the obvious to ask questions and think deeply. People are born with innate curiosity in the world around them. A sense of discovery allows people to consider new information, seek clarification, and generate new ways of doing things. According to the OECD's study on early learning and children's well-being, curiosity is strongly linked to emergent literacy and mental flexibility. A sense of curiosity leads children to be motivated to find out more information, and they are quite resourceful in figuring out how to find that information. Children's curiosity thrives in environments that not only allow for questioning and exploration but also encouragement and the promotion of opportunities for the children to express their interests. In contrast, curiosity can be suppressed when children are not given opportunities for wonder and exploration of the world around them.

According to cognitive scientist and researcher Elizabeth Bonawitz, curiosity is innate in all humans — a sensation much like hunger or thirst. "Curiosity acts as a kind of filter you put over the world to help the mind decide what information to attend to," she says. "It's a physiological response that helps drive action and decision-making to support learning." (Boudreau, 2020).

In her research, Bonawitz investigates the "wonder" aspect of curiosity — the why and the how quest for understanding rather than fact finding. Teachers can prompt a sense of curiosity by asking intentional, engaging questions such as, "What do you think happens when…?" These kinds of questions can create a more long-lasting desire for learning novel information. Children have a natural motivation to explore the world, but we can encourage a more important motivator — to explore the mind.

Reading Activities to Build Verbal Reasoning

Academic Conversations

Young students can have difficulty learning how to have an academic conversation because they may not have experience justifying their thinking to others. During an academic conversation students can learn how to question what they believe, change their minds and revise their thinking, and listen to others' perspectives, all while holding a conversation. Building these important lifelong skills is very beneficial for our young learners, and we can set up situations for our students to practice and develop these important skills.

Asking Really Good Questions

Questions can be designed to be:

- open-ended;
- something your students should care about;
- accessible to all learners (the question can be answered on many different levels);
- culturally appropriate (no person should feel uncomfortable about the content of the question).

In my experience, academic conversations can gain depth quickly with one thoughtful question asked by the teacher or a student.

For example, I did a read-aloud of the book *Shin-chi's Canoe,* by Nicola Campbell, in my grade 1 classroom. The story is about a brother and sister who were forced to leave their family and put into a residential school. The siblings had many aspects of their life taken away from them. At the end of the school year, they returned to their family.

Many of the students were making comments like,

> "If I was taken away to a residential school, I would just go to the police."
> "I would kick and punch the teachers at the school if they tried to cut my hair."
> "My parents would come and get me."

One student was quiet for a while and then asked the rest of the students, "Who would you go to if all the people we usually go to for help are the people that take us and hurt us, like police and teachers?"

The discussion then took a turn away from their current thinking and towards a social justice academic conversation. We all learned something that day.

Discuss an idea, question, or topic that involves the students directly.

When students are directly centred in a question they will often think deeply about their response.

While learning about the life cycle of butterflies with grade 3 students, I asked the question, "Where do you think we should release our butterflies?" This question led to further questions about the ecosystems, predators, and family structures of butterflies. It was determined we needed to do a lot more research in order to have an effective and successful plan for where to release our classroom butterflies.

Encourage different perspectives and even allow respectful arguments.

Students will naturally be engaged when they are given the opportunity to voice their opinions. In a math class on estimating the students in my grade 3 class were debating whether a specific jar of nickels or quarters had more value. Students were encouraged to use specific intentional language.

> I think … because …
> I agree with you because …
> I disagree with you because ….
> I notice …
> My opinion is … because …

Some students can be invited into the conversation by gently asking, "Sadie, what is your opinion about this question?" Flexible thinking and changing minds are encouraged and seen as part of the learning process.

Fiction Picture Book Lesson Activity

Photocopy a few pictures without text to give to groups of students (less than 10 percent of a book can be photocopied based on Canadian copyright laws). Have the students talk about a possible sequence of events in the story. Which picture might come first, next, etc.? Have students discuss any theories they are starting to develop. This discussion allows students to voice their ideas to others, which is empowering and motivating. It also allows students to hear different perspectives from peers and consider different possibilities. Their theories may change based on listening to others' ideas. Come back together as a whole class and have each group explain why they put their pictures in the order they did. When reading the book aloud, ask students if their ideas are confirmed, or have their theories changed, and what new information allowed them to change? This discussion permits students to change theories and encourages flexibility in thinking as they learn further information. Consider modeling the activity for students new to the process.

Wonderings about a Picture from a Text

Model curiosity building with wonderings by holding up one picture from a book and ask students, "What are you wondering about this picture?" (This can also be done with short phrases from a text.) Write down all the wonderings on the board. (Side note: I use the term wondering, rather than questions, because everyone can come up with wonderings, but not everyone has questions.) Photocopy one picture per group from the same book and have each group go through the process of writing down all their wonderings. Give students an appropriate amount of time to come up with multiple wonderings. Next, ask each group of students to choose one wondering they would like to share with the whole class. This part of the activity involves some discussion, compromise, and critical analysis. Each group will share their wondering. Because each group had different pictures, they will get a more profound sense of what the story may be about. During the reading aloud of the story, ask students how their theories are changing throughout.

Turn and Talk

A classic tried and true method of engaging our students during a read-aloud is Turn and Talk. This instructional method has stood the test of time because it is simple and effective: students have a conversation with a peer about a particular idea or topic. Turn and Talk allows students time to prepare their thinking for a whole-class or small-group discussion about a topic. The benefits include an indeterminant amount of processing time for students to try out and strengthen their thinking. Turn and Talks can be pre-planned when you have a pre-determined question to ask the class that may require time to process a response. You may choose to have a spontaneous Turn and Talk when too many voices are silent or when too many voices are clamoring to be heard at once (Nichols, 2006). A benefit of this simple method is that it requires all students to get their thinking out as they have an immediate responsibility to their partner in conversation.

Conversation Station

Setting up conversation stations is a way to bring in purposeful dialogue daily in kindergarten and grade 1 classrooms. During the interactions at the station, educators and students actively listen to each other, engage in meaningful dialogue driven by the students, and provide the opportunity for educators to develop and expand students' language.

Conversation stations provide intentional time for a conversation to happen between students and teachers.

Setting up a conversation station is quite simple but it may take some time for students to get used to the format. I would suggest choosing a quiet area of the classroom that can be a dedicated space for the conversation station. By creating comfy seating, you can give the appeal of a *coffee shop conversation setting*. The significance of the interaction is rooted in the concept that the students drive the conversation; however, most students will need to have dialogue scaffolded until they are comfortable. Teachers can accomplish this by providing some theme-related vocabulary picture cards to spark opinions or thoughts. Recently read picture books can also provide prompts for conversation starters. Establishing rules about talking and listening can be discussed with the whole class and practiced with students one-on-one. As students start to show competence and confidence in conversations, additional students may be invited to join the conversation.

There are many benefits to utilizing conversation stations in early years classrooms. A significant advantage is that educators can expand upon the language students choose to use from their background knowledge. For example, an educator may say, "You mentioned that your puppy was running into the water; was it a lake or a river? Can you tell me how your puppy looked when he was in the water?" In addition, if a student wants to tell the class about their new puppy during a whole-class discussion and there is no time to dive into the topic, the educator can suggest that the student continue the discussion during a session at the conversation station. The student feels respected and heard by the class and can be invited to be the first person at the station that day (Kelly, 2022).

Games to Strengthen Verbal Reasoning

Opposite Words

Introduce students to the idea of opposite words (or antonyms for older students). Say a word and ask the students to come up with a word that has the opposite meaning, such as dark/light, day/night. After playing the game as a whole group and modeling the process, have the students play the game in pairs, each student getting a chance to come up with a word and their partner coming up with the opposite word. For early learners, I would suggest having specific word cards for this activity; otherwise, they may come up with ambiguous words that do not have clear opposites. This game can also be played with synonyms.

Group Alike Items

Using words, picture cards, or actual items, have students individually group items that are similar into a pile. Then ask the students to explain why the items are similar, or how they are similar. Explaining will increase their vocabulary and give them time to state their thinking. As long as students provide a valid explanation, then it is correct. For instance, if a student groups picture cards for boat, train, bicycle, and car together and they explain they are all modes of transportation, they understand how the game is played and are demonstrating verbal reasoning.

First Word

This is a word association game that uses cognitive flexibility to consider how words are related to other words. Working in groups or as a whole class, one student says a word and another student says the first word that comes to mind. For example, one student says "grass", another student might say "green", or "mow", or "trees". As long as each student can explain why they said the word, they are correct. This activity is naturally differentiated and culturally responsive as there can be many ways words are associated, and at many different levels of complexity.

Categories

This is a fun, fast-paced game requiring mental agility and quick recall, so it is perfect to strengthen verbal reasoning. It can be intimidating for students who are slow processors, so you may need to differentiate it to not be a timed activity for some students. Students decide on a category and have a time limit to come up with as many words in that category as they can think of. So, if the category is "ways you can move", students may answer with words such as roll, walk, run, hop, dance, skip, jump, baby step, etc.

Guess My Word

One student comes up with a word they do not tell anyone, but instead they give clues about the chosen word and the other student(s) need to guess the word. So if the word is "chair", the student might say, "legs, back, sit…" This activity can develop in complexity if students move from items (nouns) to concepts such as biodiversity — "living things, variety, alive" — which is a great way to build content knowledge in cross-curricular lessons.

Language Structure (Syntax, Semantics, Etc.)

As babies, humans learn to understand and use oral language much earlier than they learn to read and write. When students come to school, they already have funds of knowledge in the area of language comprehension. It makes sense that teachers would use the knowledge already solidified to build new knowledge. Conversations that build on background knowledge, verbal reasoning, language structure, and theory building are an investment in students' future reading comprehension. Reading comprehension problems in later primary grades are often attributed to limited language skills and become more evident when the text complexity begins to exceed the student's language comprehension (Burkins & Yates, 2021). In order to comprehend a text, students need to understand enough words on a page to activate the language they already know.

Language structure refers to sentence-level comprehension of text, which means that the arrangement of words within sentences affects the overall meaning of the sentence. As readers, we are constantly constructing and reconstructing meanings of text using specific language structures such as syntax and semantics. Syntax is the set of rules in which words can be combined to form sentences. Semantics is the meaning of words and combinations of words.

Syntax is required for the correct use of constructing sentences so that readers can understand at the sentence level, which is critical for understanding any overall text. Language allows flexibility in how we construct sentences so students need to keep meaning in mind through working memory. Students can do this by attending to specific words that might add to the overall meaning and may further students' understanding, such as transition words or pronouns.

Semantics is related to both vocabulary and language. Vocabulary is important because students need to know individual word meanings to understand them in text. Semantics involves language as well because it allows students to consider what combinations of words mean to provide meaning within the context of the text. As with many other aspects of language, students need to be able to use words flexibly, as we already have many links between related words in our long-term memory. Rich semantic networks (words that often go together) provide opportunities for students to fill in the gaps when they are reading to further

Conversations that build background knowledge, verbal reasoning, language structure, and theory building are an investment in students' future reading comprehension.

develop comprehension. We want students to approach words with a flexible mindset so they can use the content of text to consider the overall meaning. There is more to semantics than just word meaning.

Classroom Activities That Strengthen Language Structure

Instruction at Sentence-Level Comprehension

Students need to understand who is doing what to whom. Unpacking sentences for clarity is very important for overall understanding. Consider the following sentences:

> During the baseball game, Andrea hit a home run.
> Before eating dinner, the boy did his homework.

Our sentences are not always constructed in chronological order of events. In the example about the baseball game, we can ask students, "What happened first?" In the second example, we can ask students, "Can you rephrase this sentence?" If students get the information reversed or not accurately connected, it will affect their overall understanding of the text or they may not understand other key information later in the text.

If the student is monitoring their understanding of the text (checking in with themselves to make sure everything makes sense) and finding it lacking, they may go back to the part of the text that was misunderstood and reread to adjust their overall meaning.

Getting the Gist

Nell Duke and colleagues write about the importance of explicitly teaching students "getting the gist" of a text. Teacher can explain to students that they can "ascertain key points an author intends to convey by paraphrasing, clarifying, or summarizing small portions of the text" (Duke, 2023).

Getting the gist enables students to put information into their own words.

Getting the gist of a text can help some students take some risks when explaining their responses to the text — they don't need to repeat every detail exactly. It is an important life skill for students to understand and build early in their lives, as it will help them later in life to not plagiarize and say things in their own words. Paraphrasing, clarifying, and summarizing are empowering skills to have when students realize their own words matter and are important. They have the ability to critically analyze information and decide what are the most important aspects to share with others.

Different Language in Books and Speech

One important thing to teach our students is that the language of books is often different from our language in conversation. We can point out how we use language in conversation by writing on the board verbatim what a student says when they are asking another student to play at recess. Then we can look in a book and notice the differences.

For example, you may write a student's speech as:

> "Hey, Matt, what are you doing at recess? I'm heading to the swings. Wanna come?"

You can share a page out of the book *The Recess Queen*, by Alexis O'Neill and Laura Huliska-Beith. The story is about a bully whom all the other students are afraid of during recess; they will only do or play whatever the recess queen wants. A new girl shows up at the school who doesn't know the "rules" of recess and bending to the will of the recess queen. The new girl wants to play with the recess queen and asks her to play with her.

"I like cookies, I like tea, I want you to jump with me."

By putting both the above examples on the board, you can help students notice the differences between spoken language and book language. You can continue to practice this in different contexts and with different genres of books.

It is beneficial to know that when students are reading a book they will encounter more complex or unusual words in text than when they are having conversations. We have so many different strategies to support students when encountering novel words in text. Different language structures are more diverse in text, so we can point out and discuss why an author decided to use a particular language structure and what it emphasizes in terms of the meaning.

Using language structure to derive meaning can appear seamless to the competent comprehender, and in fact we actually are consistently using these important skills automatically.

Theory of Mind

Books really are magic in that they take us into the minds of others.
Kelly Cartwright, *Executive Skills and Reading Comprehension*, 2023
(p. 253)

Oatley (2011) describes how readers construct meaning in collaboration with the author, which allows readers to develop a clear understanding of themselves and others. The collaboration provides meaningful thought processes that enhance enjoyment by engaging the mind and emotions. Oatley specifically refers to fiction as the space between the reader and author that can provide a simulation of story. He explains that, "as partners with the writer, we create a version based on our own experience of how the world appears on the surface and of how we might understand its deeper properties" (p. 18).

Theory of mind refers to a reader's theory about what's going on in a character's mind. In narrative texts, students can predict characters' actions (and understand their actions) when they analyze their motivations, intentions, and feelings and connect those to behaviors. "Reading the mind" of a character involves not just considering the actions of the character, which is what most elementary students are used to doing, but considering what the character is thinking. Considering a character's thoughts is complex thinking because it involves social understanding and an understanding of our own and other people's minds. Thoughts, feelings, intentions, motivations, and beliefs all cause people (and characters) to act in certain ways.

It may seem to students that they are "guessing" when they first start to consider a character's thoughts, but in reality they are putting some deep thinking about the character's thought processes into practice. The more students engage in this kind of thinking and discussing, the more natural the process will become.

When students become used to considering thoughts, it is an easier transition for them to consider the thought processes in themselves and the people around them. As teachers, we often teach feelings and emotions through analyzing characters in picture books. In the early years, that may involve teaching vocabulary words like frustration, embarrassment, and grief. The hope is that students will start to use that language when they are discussing their own feelings and emotions.

In later years, we can introduce students to complex ideas through books. Not only does this provide our students with increased background knowledge about humanity and the world, but it also creates space for reflection and flexible cognitive thinking.

Questions

Students need to understand that their questions would — and should be — different from many others in the classroom community, including the teacher. To prompt students to consider different questions and what they are wondering, teachers can model questions that promote deep thinking.

In the narrative book *Watercress*, by Andrea Wang, students can engage with the book and the characters at many different levels of complexity. In the story, the main character feels ashamed of her family because they drive an older car, wear second-hand clothes and, most significantly, pick watercress from the side of the road. She ducks and hides when other cars drive by to make sure she is not seen. Towards the end of the story, the main character learns that her parents grew up with very little food. The most impactful event in the story is when she learns that her uncle died from malnutrition when he was young. An interesting question to get students thinking about the main character's state of mind and how that is directly related to her actions is, Would the main character act differently if she knew about her uncle's death and what her parent's families went through at the beginning of the story? Or more simply, What changed the main character's behavior?

> Questions are as individual as the students who are asking them.

Questioning the Author

Students need to understand the fact that texts are someone's ideas written down. When students begin to relate to an author as a person who has different thoughts, ideas, and experiences from theirs they can connect more deeply with the author as a person and start to see why they may have written about a specific topic or concept. By seeing the author as a person who has written down ideas, students can share ownership for the text's meaning and consider the question, "What do you think the author is telling us?"

The conversation that develops around that question allows the class to co-create am understanding of the author's message and they can integrate that message into their existing knowledge to, perhaps, transform their thinking.

For example, I read the book *I Am Not a Penguin: A Pangolin's Lament*, by Liz Wong, to grade 3 students. Then I asked the students, "If Liz Wong were here with us right now, what questions would you have for her?"

> **Kristy:** I'm confused by the title, why didn't she just title it, *I Am a Pangolin*?
> **Molly:** I wonder why she made the other animals not like the pangolin and not listen to them?
> **Sean:** Why was the pangolin giving a presentation about themselves?

I then asked the students, "What do you think Liz Wong is trying to tell us?"

Inferencing

> Inferring gives the reader an opportunity to sense a meaning not explicit in the text, but which derives and flows from it.
> Ellin Oliver Keene and Susan Zimmerman, *Mosaic of Thought* (p. 145)

Students can be taught to develop inferences as they are reading or listening to a read-aloud. Inferencing is not a skill that comes easily to many students, so it needs to be explicitly taught and encouraged. Some students think it is "cheating" or "guessing" at what the character is thinking or what is the message in the story. Students need to be not only given permission to inference, but to have many opportunities to practice and try out this skill. Inference is part rational and part beyond definition, as it is unique to how each individual processes information. Students need to use their own creativity, life experiences, wisdom, and logic to form their own meaning in text. They need to create meaning "beyond the text to a place only he or she can go" (Keene & Zimmermann, 2007).

Teachers can explain to students that inferences are something a reader knows or concludes from reading, but the author does not include it explicitly in the book. Inferences help the reader understand the story more deeply and make meaningful connections that are very personal to the text. Simply, inferences go beyond the literal understanding for readers to add their own opinions, knowledge, and ideas to build new ideas.

During the reading of *Abdul's Story*, by Jamilah Thompkins-Bigelow, a conversation began. The story is about a boy who has lots of ideas of stories he would like to write about, but the act of writing is difficult for him. He struggles with letter formation, spelling, and making his writing readable. An author visits his class one day and encourages Abdul by showing him his own writing, which is messy and difficult to read. Abdul writes a story that the author reads in front of the class and everyone is proud of the story Abdul told through his writing.

The following is a conversation between the teacher and a student:

> **Teacher:** When Abdul was writing down his stories, I think he was feeling very discouraged. I know that is an inference because I'm using evidence from the text as well as knowledge from my own life to conclude that Abdul feels overwhelmed with the act of writing.
> **Nikoli:** I thought he was sad that he had such good stories in his mind but he couldn't share them.
> **Teacher:** You know, Nikoli, I'm interested in your inference. I want to know something. How did that inference come into your mind?
> **Nikoli:** He talked about all the stories he had about the people in his neighborhood. They sounded like such interesting people. I would want to write those stories too.
> **Teacher:** Thank you. One more question. How did that inference help you better understand the story?
> **Nikoli:** Well, it made me understand that Abdul didn't have trouble coming up with story ideas, just getting them down on paper.

Wordless Picture Books

Another way to introduce students to the process of inferencing is through wordless picture books. Students will need to rely on their thinking rather than reading words on a page to determine what is happening in the story and why. Wordless picture books can support students' exploration into theory of mind by using inferencing based on facial expressions and the non-print narrative that reveals the story. Even with older students, the power of inferencing can become concrete through the practice of reading wordless picture books.

While reading the wordless picture book titled *The Red Book*, by Barbara Lehman, my grade 3 students connected with how the main character felt depressed at the beginning of the book. The story is about a boy who is lonely and escapes into a book to find a friend. My students wrote down their thoughts on the book before we entered into an in-depth discussion.

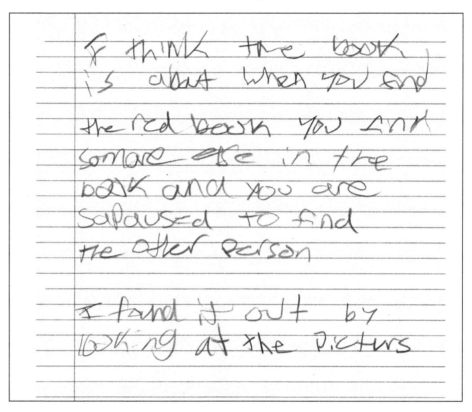

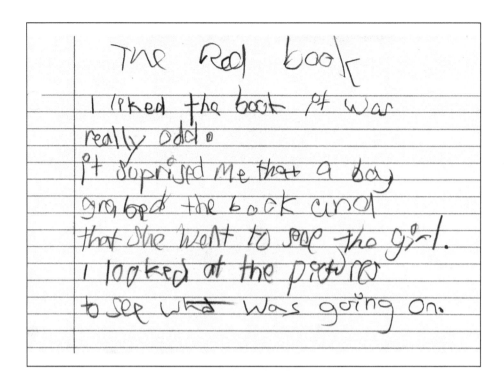

The students' initial written response was an overview of the story line; however, once we were deep in a discussion, the conversation took a deeper level of comprehension. The students used words like bleak, overwhelmed, depression, and anxiety to talk about very real emotions and how the character found friendship that helped him overcome his feelings. They used the word resilience to describe the main character's traits and how there were times in their lives that they felt emotions like the character and what they did to practice resilience themselves. We had previously been discussing social emotional learning (SEL) so some of the language was repeated as we discussed the book. Some students were ready to make a leap from talking about the character in the book to connecting to SEL competencies.

Since my students enjoyed a wordless picture book, I decided to intorduce them to a pictureless story book titled, *The Book with No Pictures* by B.J. Novak. The book is a light, fun way to engage students in a silly story with surprises on every page. Essentially, the author is making the reader say the funny words on each page, sometimes in funny voices. One page of text reads, "And now I am reading you this book with my monkey mouth and in my monkey voice." "That is not true... I am not a monkey!" I had my students choose a page out of the book to illustrate.

Blueberry
Pizza

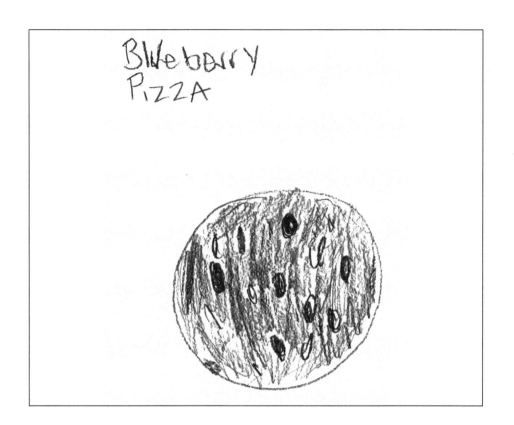

Best Kid ever

The Power of Rhetorical Questions

Rhetorical questions can be an important aspect of deep thinking and theory building when reading text. They are questions that pull readers right into the story and make them want to find out more. They are big questions that don't have a specific answer, but just thinking about them helps readers imagine a range of different possibilities within and outside of text.

Students like the idea that there are questions that do not have one correct answer.

Students may have difficulty coming up with rhetorical questions because they seem very abstract. It may be easier for students to consider fact-finding questions because of previous experience and opportunity. However, explicitly teaching students to ask rhetorical questions can be liberating for our students. They get to discover that the teacher doesn't have all the "correct" answers and the students need to supply their own. They can flex their creative muscles and go beyond what is known to be true and explore the unknown. Introduce the book *Twenty Questions*, by Mac Barnett, which outlines different kinds of questions and can get the conversation going with students as they explore the power of rhetorical questions.

In my experience, the younger the students are, the more questions they ask, including rhetorical questions. I wanted to bring back the use of immense wondering and questioning with older students. So, in a grade 5 class, we practiced coming up with questions. They were a bit shy at first, but once a few brave students spoke up, many of the others followed suit.

I used the story *Walking Together*, by Elder Albert D. Marshall and Louise Zimanyi, as a catalyst for questions. The story is about how humans, animals, and plants are all connected and how we can learn from our environment if we listen. There is an important message about the strength of walking together with others and the power of connection.

Some questions asked by students:

> **Stephanie:** The author writes about walking together in a good way. What is walking together in a bad way?
>
> **Grace:** I noticed that many words are capitalized that aren't supposed to be, like Frog, River, Willow. Why did the author do that?
>
> **Noah:** I think it means that they are a name, not a thing. Why are all the illustrations of being outside, not in a home?

The questions led to an in-depth conversation about environmentalism and what it is like living in a city rather than the country.

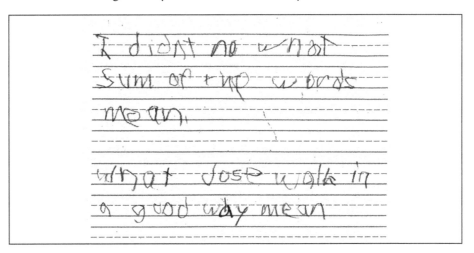

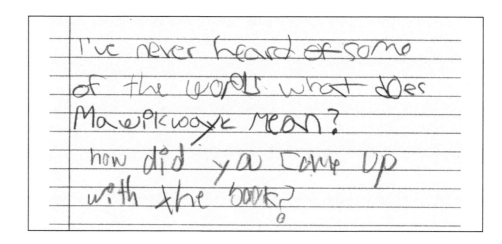

I've never heard of some of the words. what does Mawikwaye mean? how did you come up with the book?

In another case I had students write down some questions they had for the author of the book *What Do You Do with a Chance?* by Kobi Yamada. The story is essentially a rhetorical question which is explored by the main character throughout the book. The "chance" in the book nudges at the idea of being an entity of its own. The last page reads, "What do you do with a chance? You take it … because it just might be the start of something incredible."

is this book about you?

how do you know that something is a chance

how did you come up with your book? why did you write the book? Did you Draw it

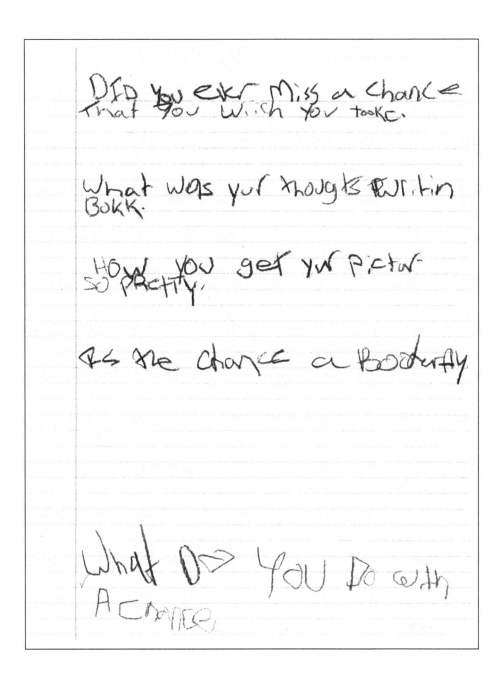

DID you ekr miss a chance
That you wish you tooke.

What was yur thougts Rwritin
Bokk.

How you get yur pictur
so pretty.

Is the chance a Booterfly

What Do you Do with
A chance.

Hands-Down Conversations

An essential skill for young children to learn and practice is to have an authentic conversation based on listening to others, adding opinions, and justifying reasons. A hands-down conversation is an opportunity for students to experience how people converse in the real world where the format of question, response, and evaluation (right or wrong) is inappropriate. In Wedekind and Thompson's book, *Hands Down, Speak Out* (2020), the authors describe the process of listening and talking through hands-down conversations. The benefits of students conversing in a high-quality dialogue are that they:

- co-create knowledge;
- question each other;
- agree or disagree with each other;

We can practice having authentic conversations with our students. That is a lifelong skill.

- look for evidence together;
- share interpretations.

The intended result is to build stronger textual understanding.

The format of hands-down conversations involves no hand raising; instead, students are taught how to listen for a place to slide their voice into the conversation. There is only one voice speaking at a time, and students are expected to listen closely to the person speaking. The teacher takes a position to the side of the students or as part of the circle to guide the conversation at times but not lead it. The teacher may prompt students by mentioning, "Sadie is trying to get her voice in. Someone can invite her by asking her what she thinks."

A beneficial way to scaffold how to share ideas and opinions in hands-down conversations is to have a detailed lesson on how to talk about reasoning or telling why you are going to say something. The teacher may begin by saying, "We are going to tell our ideas to our friends and then tell them why we think that because it will help us understand each other's thinking. We can start our sentences like: 'I think… because…', 'I noticed… so I'm thinking….'"

Here's an example of a hands-down conversation about a story in which a young girl is picked up and taken with her grandmother to live at her house in a town far away. The girl shows signs of being quite worried. Her grandmother tries to get her mind off her worries by asking her to find ten beautiful things along the drive.

> **Teacher:** Who has something they would like to say about the story *Ten Beautiful Things*, by Molly Beth Griffin?
>
> **Olivia:** I felt sad for Lily because she seemed really scared.
>
> **Graham:** Why do you think she was sad?
>
> **Olivia:** She seemed like she didn't know her Gram really well and she was talking about Gram's house being her new home. It seemed like she didn't know where she was going because she was looking at a map.
>
> **Doran:** But it is her Gram, of course she knew her. Who doesn't know their Grandma?
>
> **Brenna:** Well, I don't know my grandparents because they live in P.E.I and that's on the other side of Canada. I've only facetimed with them. They seem nice, but it would be scary going to their house all by myself.
>
> **Teacher:** It looks like Troy is trying to say something.
>
> **Brenna:** What do you think, Troy? Do you think Lily was scared?
>
> **Troy:** Yes, she kept saying her stomach hurt in the book. My stomach hurts when I'm scared.

An interesting way to monitor hands-down conversation is through conversation mapping. A teacher may draw a quick sketch of a conversation circle, noting where students are sitting, and then draw arrows to indicate where the conversation is going and who is taking part. Sharing the discussion with students afterwards and discussing what they notice about the map can lead to further reflection. After discussing who was often speaking and who was not, students become aware of the conversation directions in the following weeks and become more diligent about having an "even" conversation in which everyone is involved (Kelly, 2022).

Each of these instructional practices exposes students to new ideas, new language structures, and new vocabulary through intentional and authentic engagement in conversation. The benefits are significant and far-reaching in real-life situations. One huge benefit that needs to be addressed is the fact that all these language development opportunities set up students for enhanced reading comprehension. Reading comprehension starts long before students learn to decode; it actually begins as students learn to understand and use spoken language. The best investment in future reading comprehension is to focus on language comprehension in the early years.

"Get into the Head of the Character" Drama Activity

Have a student choose a character they want to "become" for an interview. Brainstorm what they know about the character (traits, interests, attitudes, etc.). Brainstorm with the whole class what questions the interviewer should ask the character. You want to have the student who is being interviewed to have some time to process the questions and think of possible responses. Then they can get into character and sit in the interview chair and try out the process. It is important that this activity be closely monitored and facilitated when students are beginning to familiarize themselves with the process. This kind of character analysis will not only deepen students' understanding of character development, but also improve their writing about characters.

For example:

> My grade 2 students had just completed reading aloud the book *Milo Imagines the World*, by Matt de la Peña. In the story Milo is a budding artist traveling in New York City in the subway with his older sister. He is anxious about the trip and uses his sketch pad to draw stories about the people he sees on the subway. At the end of the story, the reader finds out he and his sister were on the way to visit their mother in prison. Before we read the story together, we discussed what we knew about Matt de la Peña as an author.
>
> **Clea:** I remember that he talks a lot about feelings.
> **Stein:** Yeah, and he has an interesting way to describe feelings, so you can almost feel them in your stomach.
> **Eugene:** I wonder how he comes up with those words to describe feelings.
> **Teacher:** It's definitely a strength of his as a writer. How about we pay close attention to those great descriptions of feelings as we go through the story? If you notice a great description, put your thumb in the air.

After reading the story and stopping throughout to examine the author's descriptions of feelings and questions we had about the character and his journey, we decided to jump into further consideration about Milo.

> **Teacher:** We learned a lot about Milo throughout this story. What are some questions you would have for Milo if he were here with us in this classroom?
> **Gina:** I would ask him why his mom is in jail and how he feels about not seeing her every day.
> **Hunter:** I wonder if his sister takes care of him at home. She didn't seem very interested in him.
> **Peggi** (in a quiet voice): I wonder if he is scared for his mom being locked up. My uncle went to jail and my mom was really scared.

After we had a long list of questions for the character Milo, we took turns answering questions in the interview seat. We discussed the need to use inferences (a term they were familiar with from other lessons), because of course we had to consider what we think the character might say.

Throughout this chapter we explored different ways to invite conversation amongst students and the time and space to think deeply about text. Language comprehension generally begins to develop from birth onward, so our students have a lot of previous knowledge that benefits them when they start to further develop their language when reading. Many of the strategies outlined here can be used both with kindergarten students and with much older students.

In the next chapter I examine how different components of the AVR actually overlap with both word recognition and language comprehension to build even deeper connections through reading. Bridging processes are unique to Duke and Cartwright's (2021) model of AVR, made using current research on reading to consider the complexities that impact students' reading journeys. I will explore how print concepts, reading fluency, vocabulary knowledge, morphological awareness, and graphophonological-semantic cognitive flexibility further develop word recognition and language comprehension as our students become proficient readers.

5

Bridging Processes That Build Word Recognition and Language Comprehension

> The existence of overlap between word recognition and language comprehension in the prediction of reading is consequential for practitioners because it suggests the need to consider contributors to reading not only within word recognition and language comprehension, as in the SVR, but also across them…
>
> Nell Duke and Kelly Cartwright, *The Science of Reading Progresses: Communicating Advances Beyond the Simple View of Reading*, 2021, p. 28

The Active View of Reading model is holistic.

Word recognition and language comprehension are not entirely separate components that do not affect each other. Instead, there is significant overlap among the components and when one area is strengthened, the other benefits as well. Therefore, the AVR model is holistic, as areas of the model are strengthened and supported by other areas. In this chapter we will examine the bridging processes that influence and build proficient word recognition and language comprehension.

Print Concepts

Looking at print conceptually is a crucial part of learning to read. When students begin to notice different aspects of print, they can start to recognize how print works, how to discriminate between letters, words, and sentences, and how they are all connected. Students need to understand how to navigate reading a book. This may sound like a simple skill, but many students have difficulties with some print concepts such as directionality. Print concepts are learned skills and do not come naturally to students. Students will begin to notice how print works as they are read to and as they begin to interact with books in purposeful ways. Print concepts are considered a bridging process because they are crucial in developing word recognition skills by helping students notice letters, words, and sentences, but working with print concepts also strengthens students' knowledge of how language works when it is written down.

Students can become confused by a teacher's comments about print concepts if they do not know the "rules" of print. Most students will pick up some aspects of print concepts by watching what proficient readers do when they read books. They will begin to notice that pages are turned from right to left and the pictures match or complement the words that are spoken. If a proficient reader is pointing to the words as they read, students may notice that they are starting at a specific part of the page and going in one direction (left to right) as they read. With the rise in digital texts, it is even more important to explicitly teach students how to navigate a book in terms of how to turn pages and notice where print appears on pages.

Print concepts include the following skills.

Students can locate:

- the front of the book;
- the title of the book;
- where to begin reading;
- a letter;
- a word;
- the first word of a sentence;
- the last word of a sentence;
- the first and last word on a page;
- punctuation marks;
- a capital letter;
- a lower-case letter.

Classroom Activities That Strengthen Print Concepts

Interactive Read-Alouds

One of the most effective and natural ways we can teach students about print concepts is by modeling how to navigate print when reading to students. Teachers can explain what they are doing as they begin to read by saying:

- I'm putting my finger under the first word I need to read.
- I will stop here because this is the end of the sentence.
- I will move my finger this way (left to right) because that is the way I need to read the words on the page.
- When I get to the end of this line, I will move my finger to the beginning of the next line (return sweep).

Of course, teachers will generally focus on one skill at a time in order to not overwhelm or confuse students. Gradually introducing new print concepts as students solidify previously taught concepts will allow for a natural learning pattern.

Reading Conferences

Checking in with individual students can give teachers a sense of what print concepts students have mastered. Reading conferences give teachers the time and space to ask students questions and observe their reading behaviors, even for our youngest readers. You can do a quick assessment by asking students, Can you point to the beginning of the sentence? Can you point to a letter? A word? A capital letter? And so on. You can also have students read a few pages to see if they have voice-to-print match (if the words they are saying out loud match the words that are printed on the paper). The sooner students have an understanding of how print works, the sooner they will use their knowledge to build word recognition and language comprehension.

Known Books

Students can practice their print concepts with known or simple books. Many students can remember a lot of the words in known or simple books, or the pictures can jog their memory of what most of the words on the page are. Knowing most of the words can free up cognitive ability to think deeply about how they are reading and noticing different aspects of print. Print concept rules are difficult to master for our youngest readers, so the more modeling and practice we can give them, the better.

Reading Fluency

The more words students can recognize automatically, the more fluent they will become.

Fluency is usually associated with word recognition, but it actually has a lot to do with language comprehension as well. It is a bridging process because fluency brings together foundational skills in word reading and how students read the text to make sense of it using punctuation marks and appropriate expression. Fluency involves automatic word reading alongside prosody, the rhythm and intonation that is common when proficient readers read text. Prosody is heard when students read aloud, but it also refers to the little reading voice that we notice in our brain when we are reading silently. Reading accurately and with expression and prosody leads to reading comprehension because proficient readers are making sense of the language as they read. Fluency underpins all reading. If we do not emphasize fluency with our students, all the hard work we do in phonics lessons will not be as successful.

The more words students can recognize automatically, the more fluent they will become. Students also need to get through enough words in an appropriate time frame; otherwise, they will not be able to maintain the meaning of the text. It is helpful for students to listen to a fluent reader read aloud to understand what reading should sound like; however, students need to practice their own fluent reading in order to improve.

Weekly Plan

There is a significant amount of modeling and scaffolding needed for students to get from decoding to skilled reading. One way we can add that level of instruction on a weekly basis is to choose a grade level book and have repeated reading opportunities each day of the week. A possible schedule for repeating reading may look something like this:

Monday: Teacher reads a chosen book to students. The whole class discusses the meaning of the book and any questions that are asked.

Tuesday: Echo read. Teacher reads the text sentence by sentence modeling what fluent reading sounds like, and students repeat each sentence.

Wednesday: Choral read. Teacher and all students read the story in unison to practice fluent reading. Students who generally feel anxious when reading aloud feel a sense of safety in numbers.

Thursday: Partner read. Students partner up and decide how they would like to read the book. They may choose to read it in unison, take turns reading it page by page or sentence by sentence, or any other variation of partner reading.

Friday: Extension activity. This day the reading will depend on the book for the week. Teachers can highlight a specific aspect of the book they would like to explore further with students, or it could even be a 'Fun Friday' reading activity.

The weekly plan emphasizes that repeated readings are a way to build fluency in young readers in a safe, developmentally appropriate format. Many different genres can be read in this format for students to gain fluency with a variety of texts.

Poetry

An interesting way for students to hear and recite text while using prosody (expression and phrasing) is through poetry reading. In poetry, it is the expression and phrasing that bring meaning to the poem. Students can build word reading and language comprehension through poetry as they read the words and consider the meaning at the same time. Reading poetry also sets students up to read slowly and intentionally, rather than promoting them to read as quickly as they can.

For instance, in the book of poems *Winter Bees and Other Poems of the Cold*, by Joyce Sidman and Rick Allen, the poems are set up to encourage students to put short, impactful phrases together as they read. In the poem "Snowflake Wakes", each line adds meaning to the overall poem and is meant to be read as a phrase. The descriptions are vivid and beautifully written as snowflakes are given human qualities (personification) such as, "lace sprouting from fingertips" and "leaps, laughing". The rehearsal and performance aspect of reading poetry aloud further emphasizes reading with prosody, while drawing attention to certain aspects of the poem to focus on meaning.

Nursery Rhymes

A nursery rhyme is a short song or poem that usually conveys a message or tells a story. The sing-song format of many nursery rhymes is great for students practicing reading with prosody in a fun and engaging way. Nursery rhymes also have positive effects on working memory as students hold information in their heads while they orally rehearse. Many nursery rhymes are practiced over and over throughout the year, so the repeated readings are impactful for students who may be unfamiliar with this kind of reading. It is very difficult to read a nursery rhyme without automatically reciting in a sing-song voice. Try saying, "Mary had a little lamb," without adding expression and a lilting voice while you do. Impossible!

"Silent" Reading Does Not Exist

Student can still practice reading fluently when they are reading silently. Just because a student is reading silently, they are still "saying" the words in their head and listening to the reading internally. Fluent readers read with an emphasis on expression and phrasing as they listen to their reading. Try it! Read this text silently and notice what is happening in your brain. Do you hear the words you are saying? Try to read without expression and then with expression. Do you

The rehearsal and performance aspect of reading poetry aloud further emphasizes reading with prosody.

"hear" the difference? A great way to expose students to the concept of listening to themselves read silently is to go through this activity with them. Ask them the same questions to encourage noticing and nurturing silent reading and fluency.

Vocabulary Knowledge

Vocabulary knowledge consists of links between word spelling, pronunciation, and meaning, and those are stored in long-term memory. Vocabulary does not only mean that students know how to pronounce a word and know the meaning of the word; they also need to consider and monitor where the vocabulary word appears in writing in connected text and whether it makes sense. In the English language, we have many words that use the same spelling but have different meanings (homonyms such as *desert* and *wind*), so context is incredibly important when figuring out word meanings. Vocabulary is considered a bridging process in the Active View of Reading because students need to use their word recognition strategies alongside their language comprehension strategies.

Vocabulary can be considered a gateway to comprehend text. You cannot decode your way into learning an unknown word if you don't have any prior knowledge of the word. In my experience, vocabulary is under-addressed in elementary school and taught almost incidentally when a student asks, "What does that word mean?" In addition, sometimes teachers think they need to wait until students are reading fluently before they begin to teach vocabulary. In reality, there is a direct connection between vocabulary, word knowledge, and reading comprehension: students need to know enough words to understand a text, then they can spend a bit of their time trying to figure out the meaning of any unknown words. The challenge comes when students do not know enough words to comprehend the text or get the gist of it; then it is going to be very difficult to comprehend the overall meaning.

To know a word means having a lot of information about it. Students need to know:

- what the word means in their own words (not a dictionary definition);
- words that mean something similar (synonyms);
- multiple meanings of the word;
- morphological knowledge;
- spelling and phonological knowledge of the word.

Read-Alouds to Build Vocabulary
A read-aloud experience is a learning event in which all the students in the class celebrate and learn from a text as the teacher reads to students. Students listen, notice, wonder, and discuss their reactions and ideas with classmates. Typically, as the teacher is reading, they may pause and pose questions at important parts of the text to have students engage in collaborative conversations to help them explore the meaning and/or message of the text (Walther, 2019).

In addition, there are a number of compelling reasons to read aloud, according to Maria Walther (2019). It:

- promotes reading;
- fosters a strong sense of community;
- celebrates the written word;

- expands vocabulary;
- showcases a proficient reading strategy use;
- supports budding writers;
- encourages perspective taking and empathy;
- opens windows to other worlds.

Students need to be taught that reading is an action sport, but the action takes place in their minds.

Read-alouds are a beneficial way to build vocabulary knowledge within a connected text experience. Generally, teachers choose books for read-alouds that are at a significantly higher text complexity than students are able to read, so they get exposure to deeper thinking opportunities.

Consider the following tips when planning a read-aloud:

When planning read-alouds, read the book beforehand and come up with focus areas.

- Read the book ahead of time and plan the words you will want to give students more information about during the reading.
- Plan to revisit words that you think are important to spend more time on discussing.
- Plan out ways you can actively discuss an unfamiliar word (e.g., acting it out, discussing multiple meanings, using the word in different ways, putting the word in different contexts).
- When you are doing a read-aloud, you can still give quick child-friendly definitions in the moment as you read a word students may not know. It is helpful for students to understand that word in the particular context of the book. If they don't understand it in context, it probably will not be enough for that word to be stored in long term memory with all the knowledge needed to fully understand a word.

Generally, we want our students to be strategic because we cannot teach them every single word. Rather than teaching them one strategy to rely on, we want them to think about multiple strategies and see what works for them in this situation. That way students gain much more independence. We therefore want our students to know a lot about how words work and how we gain knowledge about therm.

There are three main ways in which we learn new words:

1. through texts;
2. when we try new activities (e.g., fishing: we learn topic-specific words such as bait, tackle, cast, rod, angling, etc.);
3. through oral language interactions (this is how we learn the most words). This means that we learn words used in our environment, so the more often sophisticated words are used in our environment, the more they will become part of our vocabulary.

In my grade 2 class, we were studying rocks and minerals. One day, some students came back from recess saying they were confused because they had found a piece of basalt in the playground and they hadn't thought they would find one in the area because we were in the mountains and not anywhere near volcanoes. They explained they knew that basalt is formed from metal-rich lava as it cools. That began a very interesting conversation about the earth and built even more vocabulary knowledge. The more specialized or interesting words we use around students, the more opportunities they have to learn them. As you can see from the learning around rocks and minerals, vocabulary learning supports all curricular learning areas, not just language arts. Our students need to comprehend across many subject areas throughout the day.

Vocabulary can and should be pre-planned to be ready so as not to miss opportunities; however, giving students a list of vocabulary words to learn or memorize at the beginning of a unit can be overwhelming and counterproductive to the deep learning that needs to happen. It is not a meaningful context for word learning.

Nell Duke and colleagues wrote a blog titled *Looking to Research for Literacy Success* (2023).

The researcher outlined ten "Significant Ways to Build Knowledge through Language":

1. Build in opportunities for children to develop oral language from birth by creating language-rich environments that build knowledge and motivate children to want to learn to read.
2. Grow vocabulary through exposure to informational read-alouds.
3. Have discussions that promote intentional student dialogue.
4. Read aloud books that have more complex ideas and vocabulary than what students can read on their own.
5. Teach word reading and spelling so students can build content knowledge through reading.
6. Apply strategies for making sense of text that increase cognitive engagement.
7. Build on students' interests and curiosity to maximize cognitive engagement.
8. Plan teaching content from the curriculum as it is already coherently sequenced.
9. Introduce students to a variety of genres to widen their knowledge of places, times, and topics.
10. Use Science and Social Studies instruction to help build literacy skills.

Learning New Content-Specific Words

The big question is: How we can support students to transfer words into their long-term memory so they become part of the students' vocabulary? One way is to look at words in different contexts and discover interesting aspects of the content words. Marcia Tate (2016) describes some strategies for making words stick with students. I pulled the following important words that students need to know and understand from the British Columbia Curriculum: landforms, ecosystems, thermal energy, and biodiversity.

Word Explosion

Teachers can put the word *landforms* in the middle of a whiteboard. Ask students: What do you notice about this word? Student responses may include, I notice there are two words, land and forms; I notice that this word might be something about things found on the land; I recognize that the word forms might be something to do with the forms I fill out at the dentist.

Acknowledge the responses from students and tell them that landforms are natural features of the earth's surface.

Give students the beginning letters of some words that are landforms and see if they can come up with the different landforms you've started to write.

mou-
hi-
plat-
val-
riv-
del-
gla-

Give students some time to come up with as many words as they can and then ask for their answers once everyone has written them down: e.g., mountain, hill, plateau, valley, river(bed), delta, glacier.

Later in the lesson, say you have a pop quiz for the students. Ask them to write down their definition of landforms and then write down three different examples of landforms. By revisiting and reviewing the concept, you increase the chance that the vocabulary words will be more prominent in the students' minds.

Word Part Exploration

Teachers write the word *biodiversity* on the whiteboard and then write bio and diversity on either side of the whole word to separate them.

Ask students: What do you notice about the beginning of the word biodiversity — bio? Once students share their initial noticings, ask them if they know any other words that start with bio-. They may answer with words like biology, biographical, biography. Tell students that all those words have something to do with "life".

Ask students: What do you notice about the end of the word biodiversity — diversity? Students will probably connect to different concepts of the word such as differences, variety, inclusion of differences. Tell students that all those words have something to do with the word "various".

Ask students: Think about what we know about the meaning of these two parts of the word. What do you think the word biodiversity means? Students may answer with something like "the variety of different types of living things".

Later in the lesson, say you have a pop quiz for the students. Ask them to write down their definition of biodiversity and what bio- means and what diversity means. The focus on morphological awareness will support students to remember the word, its meaning, plus the two parts of the word and their meanings.

Acting Out Words

Acting out words is a fun, engaging way for students to focus on word meaning and concepts. Teachers write the term *thermal energy* on the whiteboard.

Ask students: What do you notice about the term thermal energy? After students' input, explain that thermal energy is the energy that comes from the movement of particles within matter. Depending on what students have already learned, you may need to revisit the meanings of particles and matter before this lesson.

Explain to students: Sometimes the movement of particles is fast and sometimes it is slow. Ask students: Do you think the movement of particles would be fast or slow when you have a pot of boiling water on the stove? Fast. What about if you are watching an ice cube melt? Slow.

Tell students you are going to act out being a particle. Have the students stand up and explain they can move their arms and legs and bodies quickly to show the movement when a pot of water is boiling. Then have them practice moving their bodies slowly when an ice cube is melting. Ask the students to listen carefully when you say either pot boiling or ice cube melting and match their actions to the words you say. Depending on the students you have in front of you, you may want to have them show you particle movement by gently bumping into the students around them. But, if this gets out of control, just stick to the students moving their bodies in place.

Topic Text Sets

Using text sets is beneficial for this activity. Have various books at different reading levels and text formats for students to give them a choice. Model the process with the whole group by asking, "We are going to read a book about orcas. What vocabulary words do you expect to see in this book?" Make a list on the board (killer whales, migration, pods, black and white, communication, ocean, etc.). Then read the book after explaining to the students that they can clap their hands every time they hear a word from the list on the board. This activity will encourage students to listen carefully and be further engaged in the text. After reading the book, ask students: What words did we miss on our list? What can we add to our list? Then students can choose a book to go through the process in small groups. You may have text sets of books on a similar topic to the one you modeled, such as aquatic animals. As a further writing connection, when students finish going through the process above, have them individually choose five critical words or phrases they came up with and do some writing about their aquatic animal (this can take the form of a few sentences, a paragraph, a drawing with a caption, a magazine cover, a diagram, etc.).

Concept Text Sets

Students can build knowledge on key concepts across different texts. The difference between topics and concepts can be described by the knowledge we want our students to gain.

> **Topic:** seasons
> **Concept:** a specific idea we want our students to learn about seasons, such as life cycle of trees

Students will pick up more vocabulary related to the concept and even pick up other incidental vocabulary when they are exposed to multiple forms of text (e.g., diagrams, photographs, articles, videos, podcasts, print in a variety of formats and text complexity, etc.)

Concept Word Sorts

Concept word sorts are easily differentiated.

Depending on what you are teaching, you can introduce your students to a concept by sorting words into categories. With your youngest learners, you may provide picture word cards that feature both a picture and the word for something. For example, for a class studying the habitat of animals, you can create a T-chart with the words *animals that live in water* on one side and *animals that live on land* on the other side. Students then use a variety of picture cards they can sort into the two categories.

Some interesting conversations about habitat may come up as students encounter picture word cards for geese or frogs. The realization that there may be animals that live both in water and on land can prompt some further discussion and greater understanding of the concept.

Morphological Awareness

Teachers cannot possibly teach every single English word to their students, but we can teach our students some strategies that will help them learn words on their own as they encounter them in text. Morphological awareness refers to having knowledge of the smallest meaningful units of language, such as in unhelpful (un-, -help-, -ful). Morphemes are the building blocks of meaning which not only represent sounds but represent the connections between words. Morphological awareness is a bridging process in the AVR because it shows the connection between word recognition and language comprehension. The English language can be tricky, so we can let our students in on a secret: they will learn the "system" or "code" for written language, but they can't expect perfection all the time. We need to have some level of flexibility when considering the patterns of language. However, a way to increase our students' knowledge and independence is to invite our students into a culture where they can see what reading can do for them.

Correct Terminology

Teach students what the base of the word is (help), the prefix (un-), and the suffix (-ful). The base is the most important part of the word because it provides us with the most meaningful aspect of the word. The main part of the word needs to be very clear to students and should be identified and discussed first.

You may want to begin word analysis by putting a box around the base word and continue to use that method of identification so students do not get confused.

For example:

> Find the base in these words…
>> reading
>> reader
>> reread
>> reads

When considering which prefixes and suffixes to teach our early learners, the most commonly found in children's books are:

> Prefixes: un- (not), re- (again), im- in- il- ir- (not)

> Suffixes: -s, -es (plural of noun), -ed (past tense of verb), -ing (verb tense)

Students may not transfer their learning when reading and writing text, so we can provide lots of practice and encouragement to use what they are learning in real-life applications.

Try oral practice of different ways to use a base word:

You can give students a base and some different suffixes and see what they can come up with to build words and notice what happens to the meaning of each word.

Orally, we can practice building sentences that use different suffixes such as:

- I talked with my mom last night.
- I prefer talking on the phone to texting.
- My brother is quite a talker.
- Mrs. Kelly talks and talks and talks.

Act Out the Word

You can introduce this activity to the whole class with some modeling and guided practice. When students seem to be developing some independence with the format, you can easily move this activity into a literacy station. It can also be a small-group lesson to give students extra practice.

Have the students look at a set of word cards and practice acting out the action words. First, act out a word — say, *tie* (as in tie a knot in the string). Second, act out the word *untie* (untie the knot in the string). Next, act out the word *retie* (using the string to retie the knot). This activity works well if you have some props.

Using blocks, act out the word *stack*, then *unstack*, and finally *restack*.

See if students can think of an action word to act out with different suffixes.

Odd One Out

Students will start to notice how they can manipulate words and different aspects of words. You can quickly choose four words and put them on the board and ask students, "Which one doesn't belong with the others?"

bus	ties
walks	talks

Giving students time to practice noticing morphology for meaning and vocabulary words will not only increase their ability to recognize more words and consider their meaning within context, it may also improve their spelling.

Different Kinds of Texts

As noted, it is beneficial for students to see and read a variety of texts in the classroom. Different genres use text differently and introduce students to new words and sentence structures. We can introduce our students to literature, information books, and graphic novels, to name just a few. There is no perfect text to teach everything we need to learn about text and encountering new words; instead, we can rely on many different texts to teach different aspects of reading. In addition, students will benefit from seeing the same word in different texts in order to gain a well-rounded understanding of the word used in different contexts. When studying plants, students may see the word *soil* used to describe where vegetables grow, what is needed to nurture the earth, and perhaps where animals have homes.

Tying Morphology and Phonics Together

A possible lesson structure to emphasize how morphology is related to phonics as a bridging process can look something like this:

1. Meaning. Let's look at the base word and discuss what it means. Turn to your elbow partner and say this word in a sentence.
2. Examine. Match sound-spellings to consider what are regular sound-spellings and which we need to memorize by heart.
3. Practice. Let's play with the word now. Can we add any prefixes or suffixes to make more English words?

It is more beneficial for students to recognize a base word, then prefixes and suffixes, rather than to find random little words in longer words. When students focus on finding the base word, they are focused on the meaning, which will help them understand the meaning. If we consider a word such as *uneaten*, we can notice little words like *ten*, *neat*, and *ate*, but none of those words are going to help students figure out the meaning of the larger word and how to pronounce it correctly.

The purpose of focusing on morphology is so students do not feel like they have to learn each word individually. Students can find connections between words and realize their learning has just increased exponentially because of learning one new root word.

Graphophonological-Semantic Cognitive Flexibility (Letter-Sound-Meaning Flexibility)

Graphophonological-semantic cognitive flexibility — that is a mouthful! The term refers to the ability to process both the spoken parts of words and the meanings of those words. When students can think flexibly about graphophonology (the written or printed representation of sounds) and semantics (meanings) and can actively switch back and forth between sounds and meanings of printed words, then they will have more knowledge and understanding of the English language.

In many classrooms decoding sounds and understanding the meanings of words and sentences are assessed separately; however, there is a connection between sound-meaning understandings and executive functioning skills like cognitive flexibility and working memory. When students use sound-meaning flexibly, the process will contribute to their overall reading comprehension.

Many students in our early learning classrooms are taught letter-sound connections first, and then they focus on meaning. Students who are struggling with reading comprehension often have weaker semantic activation (making meaning) of written words (Cartwright, 2023).

From the simplest text, such as *Gossie and Gertie*, by Olivier Dunrea, children can learn that reading is about making meaning. As children read simple books describing different enjoyable ways friends play together (example: "Follow me! cried Gossie. Gossie marched to the barn. Gertie followed."), they can consider what that text means to them as individuals and start developing their own ideas about how they might play with their friends. This act of ownership puts reading in the child's hands and allows them to discover that reading is an interaction between the reader and the author. They do not need to be passive recipients of text (or word callers). Instead, they can begin to consider what this book is about, what I can learn from this book, what may come next in this book, how might this knowledge affect my life?

Such discovery can be encouraged by asking children questions as they read. What activities do you like to do with your friends? What do you expect to learn from this book? What activities were left out of this book? What message is the author trying to tell us?

Some other activities to boost sound-meaning connections with our beginning readers, outside of connected text, can be modeled as a whole group and then practiced in small group intervention lessons or literacy stations, based on what your students need to be successful.

Organizing Cut-Up Sentences

Cut-up sentences are also beneficial when teaching print concepts.

You can model how to write out sentences (written through interactive writing with the whole class) and then cut up the sentences into individual words. Students' working memory will be activated as they remember the words in the sentence and hold the meaning of the sentence in their thinking. You can guide students to assist in saying the sentence and finding the corresponding words to put the sentence back in order. This process also assists left-right directionality, the fact that spaces need to come between words, and the knowledge of using capitals and punctuation correctly.

Categorizing Words

Students can learn different ways to categorize words that will help them notice and analyze different aspects of word sounds and word meanings. There are many ways students can sort words, such as by:

- words that have the same beginning sound;
- words that have similar meanings;
- words that are action words (verbs) and object words (nouns).

Students can choose how to categorize words and explain in their own words how they chose to categorize.

Morning Message

Many primary classrooms use a morning message for different aspects of learning. Not only does the morning message bring together the classroom community to consider what events will be happening in the classroom or school that day, but the actual message is a tool for teaching beginning reading and writing. A great way to involve students in the creation and reading of the message is to write it on the board as a cloze passage, where some of the sounds or words are missing and the students can work together to figure out the missing parts by considering the sounds in words and the meanings of words.

Sample Morning Message:

Good M__n___ Friends!
Tod__ we are go___ to meet our buddy class outside.
We will br___ our books with us. You can read your _____ to your b_g buddy.
Enjoy the sunsh_n_ tod__!

When students start to consider sounds and meanings at the same time (and flexibly), they can integrate these skills when reading connected text, which improves reading comprehension.

Bridging processes are an important part of the AVR model because they develop both word recognition skills and language comprehension, so they are considered high value. Many of the strategies shared in this chapter involve examining an aspect of language (such as morphological awareness or vocabulary) and then practicing word solving strategies within connected text. The bridging processes help students develop an understanding for how language works when it is written down.

The final chapter will bring the different facets of the AVR model together. We will explore ways that we can look holistically at reading instruction and notice all the areas of the AVR model present in some basic instructional practices.

6

Bringing It All Together in the Classroom

How do the components of the Active View of Reading build comprehension?

Consider the following information text I wrote for the purposes of this book:

> Lakes are the best body of water to go swimming. The water is cool and clean. Sometimes you can see salmon **spawning** and **gaggles** of geese swimming by. My dad says swimming in a lake is better than swimming in a pool because you can open your eyes under water. The water looks sparkly when the sun hits it. If it is a windy day, you might experience waves. It is always fun to move with the rhythmic motion as the waves toss you around.

So much learning can happen within a single paragraph.

Now let's consider it within the scope of the different components we learned about in the first five chapters of this book.

Word Recognition

The majority of word recognition components are used for early reading development, and then they are revisited when students need to use strategic action to solve unknown words. This text is beyond a beginning text and is not decodable; instead, we will use many other components to build meaning while reading accurately.

In such a text, I could focus on a phonics skill such as vowel teams. By examining words like *cool, pool, geese,* and *clean,* students can work on their knowledge of vowel teams and then blend those sounds with others and decode the words. These words help students to develop meaning for the overall text.

There are many words that students will recognize because they are high-frequency words like *are, the, is, you, to,* and *with.* These words will help with the sentence structure and flow of the writing in order for it to make sense and sound right.

In addition, there are some complex words, such as *experience, waves,* and *toss,* that require more comprehension to understand what the words mean within the context of the paragraph.

A single approach to word recognition is not helpful when students need many skills working together to read enough words on the page to develop meaning and understand how the words work together to further acquire overall understanding, which results in knowledge building.

Morphological Knowledge

Students gain a morphological understanding of words when they are able to analyze parts of words and build on the base of the word, which helps students recognize and understand a variety of words. In the paragraph above, the word *swimming* is essential to the overall meaning of the text. Students can focus on the suffix *-ing* to think about the word as an action word which is referred to repeatedly in the text and requires understanding.

The words *sparkly* and *windy* are similar types of words that students may point out as descriptive words, or adjectives. Students may notice the *-y* at the end of the word that is consistent with what they probably know about many describing words.

Morphological knowledge builds along with text complexity; therefore, it is important to teach morphological awareness to younger and older students as they read more complex texts. Students may come across a word like *incomprehensibly* and consider what they already know about morphology to gain an understanding of the word.

Fluency

When students accurately decode words in texts, or if they know the word meaning from previous knowledge, they can gain understanding of the connected text. More cognitive attention can be spent on gaining a deep understanding of the text as working memory holds on to continuous meaning. Reading with prosody (expression and phrasing) means students are grouping words that make sense together, such as *body of water, salmon spawning, gaggles of geese,* and *rhythmic motion,* which further supports comprehension.

Vocabulary

Knowledge of the words *spawning* and *gaggles* is likely determined by each student's previous knowledge of salmon and geese. Scaffolded support to students who lack the necessary background knowledge to understand the text can be provided in the form of oral discussions before reading the text and specific word instruction through orthographic mapping and analysis of the new vocabulary words.

Graphophonological-Semantic Cognitive Flexibility

Remember, this mouthful of a phrase refers to letter-sound-meaning flexibility. We want to teach students that they need to approach words flexibly and be ready to consider the meaning of the text to support how they are using sounds to decode words.

In the paragraph at the beginning of this chapter there are some words that have multiple meanings depending on the context they are written in within connected text.

- A "*body* of water" may be an unusual phrase for students depending on their background knowledge about large expanses of water, so they may need to approach it with an understanding that the body probably does not refer to a human body.
- "When the sun *hits* it" refers to *touches* and not hand-to-hand combat.
- "Waves *toss* you around" may sound strange if students are thinking of *tossing* a baseball.
- "Experience *waves*" in a lake due to wind and currents is very different from waving goodbye to someone.

Reading-Specific Background Knowledge

Reading comprehension does not consist of only listening comprehension and word recognition because there are features of written text that are not evident in an oral-only environment.

Punctuation marks signal what is happening in connected text and how the reader interprets the meaning. An ellipse signals a dramatic pause and generally indicates that something surprising or emphasized is going to happen within the text. An exclamation point requires an emphasis on what was just read previous to the punctuation mark.

Instructional text features help the reader navigate a text to determine important information. Text features may include diagrams, photos, titles and subtitles, bolded words, table of contents, and glossaries. In our paragraph above two words are bolded (**spawning**, **gaggles**), which signals to the reader there will be more information about those words somewhere in the book. Also, the language structure in the sentence *My dad says swimming in a lake is better than swimming in a pool because you can open your eyes under water* sets the reader up for comparing and contrasting, which can support processing the information.

Cultural and Other Content Knowledge

We can provide explicit instruction on how to think about text before, during, and after reading.

A significant amount of a student's comprehension of the above paragraph depends on their background knowledge about swimming in lakes. If a student has never swam in a lake or seen a lake, it would be difficult to start to put together concepts such as waves, opening eyes under water, salmon spawning, and geese swimming by. I imagine the lack of such background knowledge would for some children be comparable to my lack of knowledge of living in a desert; I might need help understanding a paragraph about that subject. For students without any background knowledge, additional supports may be necessary for basic comprehension. Photographs, videos, diagrams, and lots of conversation would be helpful for students before, while, and after reading the text.

We can provide explicit instruction on how to think about text before, during, and after reading. We also want students to monitor their own understanding and use strategies when they begin to struggle with meaning (Duke, Ward, & Pearson, 2021).

Integrate reading throughout the week to build and develop an Active View of Reading

To develop active, purposeful, thinking readers we can set our students up for a successful reading experience that brings many aspects of the AVR together through a five-day plan for shared reading.

Monday: understanding the text
Tuesday: phonemic awareness and phonics
Wednesday: vocabulary
Thursday: fluency
Friday: oral or written response

I will describe the process I worked through with my grade 1 students using the book *Llama Llama Red Pajama*, written by Anna Dewdney. The story is about a baby llama who is going to bed and gets quite concerned that his mother is not coming in to say goodnight. He shows his feelings by yelling and crying until his mom comes into his room to calm him down.

Monday: shared reading mini-lesson about the main character

I explained to students that thinking about a character (or setting or major event) can help them better understand what they read in the story.

(see template, pg 115)

Created an anchor chart.

Describe Character	Character actions (WHY?)	Character Feelings (WHY?)

I read the story aloud pausing at pre-determined parts to think with students about the main character (Llama Llama). Together we added writing to the anchor chart based on what the students said about the character.

Describe Character	Character actions (WHY?)	Character Feelings (WHY?)
baby has a mama sleeps in a bed wears pajamas dramatic	screaming crying yelling hugging	scared lonely worried affectionate

Tuesday: shared reading with a focus on phonemic awareness and phonics

I asked the students what they remembered about the language used in the book from yesterday. They mentioned repeated words like *mama, llama, pajama*. I

It is helpful to refer to your sound wall as you examine sound-spelling patterns.

wrote the words on the board. "Let's look closely at these words and figure out what is similar."

We read through the story again, noticing where there were rhyming words and I wrote the rhyming pairs on the board for further analysis when we finished the story. We discussed sound-spellings of the rhyming pairs and noted when the words rhymed but did not have matching sound-spellings.

Wednesday: vocabulary shared reading

I said that we were going to be word detectives that day and find all the interesting words in the story. The students and I co-created some criteria for what makes a word interesting. The criteria we came up with were: You do not hear it often and many students agree that it is *interesting*. Every time I said an interesting word, students were to put their thumb up in the air. We would write the interesting words on the board for further analysis after we finished reading.

The list included words like *fret, hums, tune, whimpers, moan, pouts, weeping, wailing, tizzy, drama*. We noticed that many of the words we wrote down were action words, so we sorted the action words into one column and started to act them out. Then we picked out which words had a suffix and put a box around the base word and a circle around the suffix.

Thursday: fluency

I explained that the way this book was written was almost musical because of all the rhyming words. We practiced echo reading each page as I modeled how each line of text was meant to be said as a phrase.

After we practiced echo reading as a whole group, students practiced phrasing lines in pairs reading one page out of the book that was photocopied for practice purposes.

Friday: oral or written response

I explained that students could either make an iPad book recommendation video or a written book recommendation about this story. I encouraged them to include details they liked about the book and give it a star rating.

The five-day lesson with the same book is a good representation of the different facets of the AVR featured in the many different components of reading together through repeated, shared reading.

Reading can seem effortless to competent, skilled comprehenders, but there is nothing further from the truth. There are so many things happening in our students' brains, and our brains as proficient readers, that the whole process really is amazing. Years of teaching students to read have brought me a renewed sense of awe that I was able to be a part of students' reading journeys and a witness to their development as proficient readers.

> To read slowly is to maintain an intimate relationship with a writer. If we are to respond to a writer, we must be responsible. We commit ourselves to follow a train of thought, to mentally construct characters, to follow the unfolding of an idea, to hear a text, to attend to language, to question, to visualize scenes.
> Thomas Newkirk, *The Art of Slow Reading*, 2012, p. 2

Throughout this book I have referred to student's reading as a journey. The quote above describes what readers engage in throughout their lives, as we continue to develop as readers and thinkers. As teachers, we have the honour and responsibility to be a great part of our students' journeys that will continue to benefit them throughout their lives. My hope is that you pride yourself on the important role you have in many students' lives and the fact that your efforts have a profound impact. Enjoy this learning journey and take time along the way to slow down and celebrate.

Thought Bubbles

Sound Boxes

Word Ladders

Portable Word Wall

Aa	**Bb**
Cc	**Dd**
Ee	**Ff**
Gg	**Hh**
Ii	**Jj**
Kk	**Ll**

Pembroke Publishers ©2023 *Active Reading Classrooms: strategies that build language comprehension and word recognition skills* by Jennifer Kelly ISBN 978-1-55138-365-1

Portable Word Wall (continued)

Mm	Nn
Oo	**Pp**
Qq	**Rr**
Ss	**Tt**
Uu	**Vv**
Ww	**Xx, Yy, Zz**

Pembroke Publishers ©2023 *Active Reading Classrooms: strategies that build language comprehension and word recognition skills* by Jennifer Kelly ISBN 978-1-55138-365-1

T-Chart

What do you see?	What does this make you wonder?

Character Development

Describe Character	Character Actions (WHY?)	Character Feelings (WHY?)

Pembroke Publishers ©2023 *Active Reading Classrooms: strategies that build language comprehension and word recognition skills* by Jennifer Kelly ISBN 978-1-55138-365-1

Resources

Aukerman, M. & Schuldt, L. (2021). "What Matters Most? Toward a Robust and Socially Just Science of Reading." *Reading Research Quarterly, 56*(S1), S85-S103.

Boudreau, E. (2020). "A Curious Mind: How Educators and Parents Can Encourage and Guide Children's Natural Curiosity — in the Classroom and at Home." *Usable Knowledge*, Harvard Graduate School of Education. https://www.gse.harvard.edu/news/uk/20/11/curious-mind

Burkins, J. & Yates, K. (2021). *Shifting the Balance.* Stenhouse Publishers, Portsmouth, New Hampshire.

Butler, D., Schnellert, L., & Perry, N. (2017). *Developing Self-Regulating Learners.* Pearson, Toronto, CA.

Cartwright, K. (2023). *Executive Skills and Reading Comprehension (2nd ed.).* The Guilford Press, New York.

Cruz, M. C. (2019). *Writers Read Better: Narrative.* Corwin, Thousand Oaks, CA.

Duke, N. (2023). "Looking to Research for Literacy Success." www.ascd.org/blogs/looking... https://t.co/9aHJymzKyY

Duke, N. & Cartwright, K. (2021). "The Science of Reading Progresses: Communicating Advances beyond the Simple View of Reading." *Reading Research Quarterly, 56*(S1).

Duke, N., Ward, A., & Pearson, D. (2021). "The Science of Reading Comprehension Instruction." *The Reading Teacher, 74*(6).

First Nations Education Steering Committee (2020). *In Our Own Words: Bringing Authentic First Peoples Content to the K-3 Classroom.* FNESC, Vancouver, Canada.

OECD (2021). Is curiosity a key to better early learning? OECD Education and Skills Today. June 14, 2021. https://oecdedutoday.com/curiosity-key-better-early-learning/#:~:text=It%20is%20certainly%20easier%20to,original%20ways%20of%20doing%20things.

Johnston, P. H. (2012). *Opening Minds: Using Language to Change Lives.* Stenhouse Publishers, Portsmouth, NH.

Johnston, P. H. et al (2020). *Engaging Literate Minds: Developing Children's Social, Emotional, and Intellectual Lives, K-3.* Stenhouse Publishers, Portsmouth, NH.

Keene, E. O. & Zimmerman, S. (2007). *Mosaic of Thought: The Power of Comprehension Strategy Instruction* (2nd ed.). Heinemann, Portsmouth, NH.

Kelly, J. (2022). "Language Comprehension for the Early Years." *Teacher Magazine*, British Columbia Teachers' Federation.

MacKay, S. H. (2021). *Story Workshop: New Possibilities for Young Writers.* Heinemann, Portsmouth, NH.

Miller, D. (2009). *The Book Whisperer: Awakening the Inner Reader in Every Child.* Jossey-Bass, San Francisco, CA.

Newkirk, T. (2012). *The Art of Slow Reading.* Heinemann, Portsmouth, NH.

Nichols, M. (2006). *Comprehension through Conversation: The Power of Purposeful Talk in the Reading Workshop.* Heinemann, Portsmouth, NH.

Scoggin, J. & Schneewind, H. (2021). *Trusting Readers: Powerful Practices for Independent Reading.* Heinemann, Portsmouth, New Hampshire.

Speer, N.K., Reynolds, J.R., Swallow, K., & Zacks, J.M. (2009). "Reading Stories Activates Neural Representations of Visual and Motor Experience." *Psychological Science, 20,* 989–999.

Tate, M. (2016). *Worksheets Don't Grow Dendrites (3rd ed.).* Corwin, Thousand Oaks, CA.

Wedekind, K. O. & Thompson, C. H. (2020). *Hands Down Speak Out: Listening and Talking Across Literacy and Math K-5.* Stenhouse Publishers, Portsmouth, New Hampshire.

Willms, H. & Alberti, G. (2022). *This Is How We Teach Reading... And It's Working.* Pembroke Publishers, Markham, Ontario.

Whitehurst, G. (2015). "Dialogic Reading: An Effective Way to Read to Preschoolers." Reading Rockets. https://www.dyslexicadvantage.org/wp-content/uploads/2016/10/Dialogic-Reading-An-Effective-Way-to-Read-to-Preschoolers-Reading-Rockets.pdf

Young, C., Paige, D., & Raskinski, T. (2022). *Artfully Teaching the Science of Reading.* Routledge, New York, NY.

Index